ROY BENNETT

Listening to Music

LONGMAN

Lives of the Composers

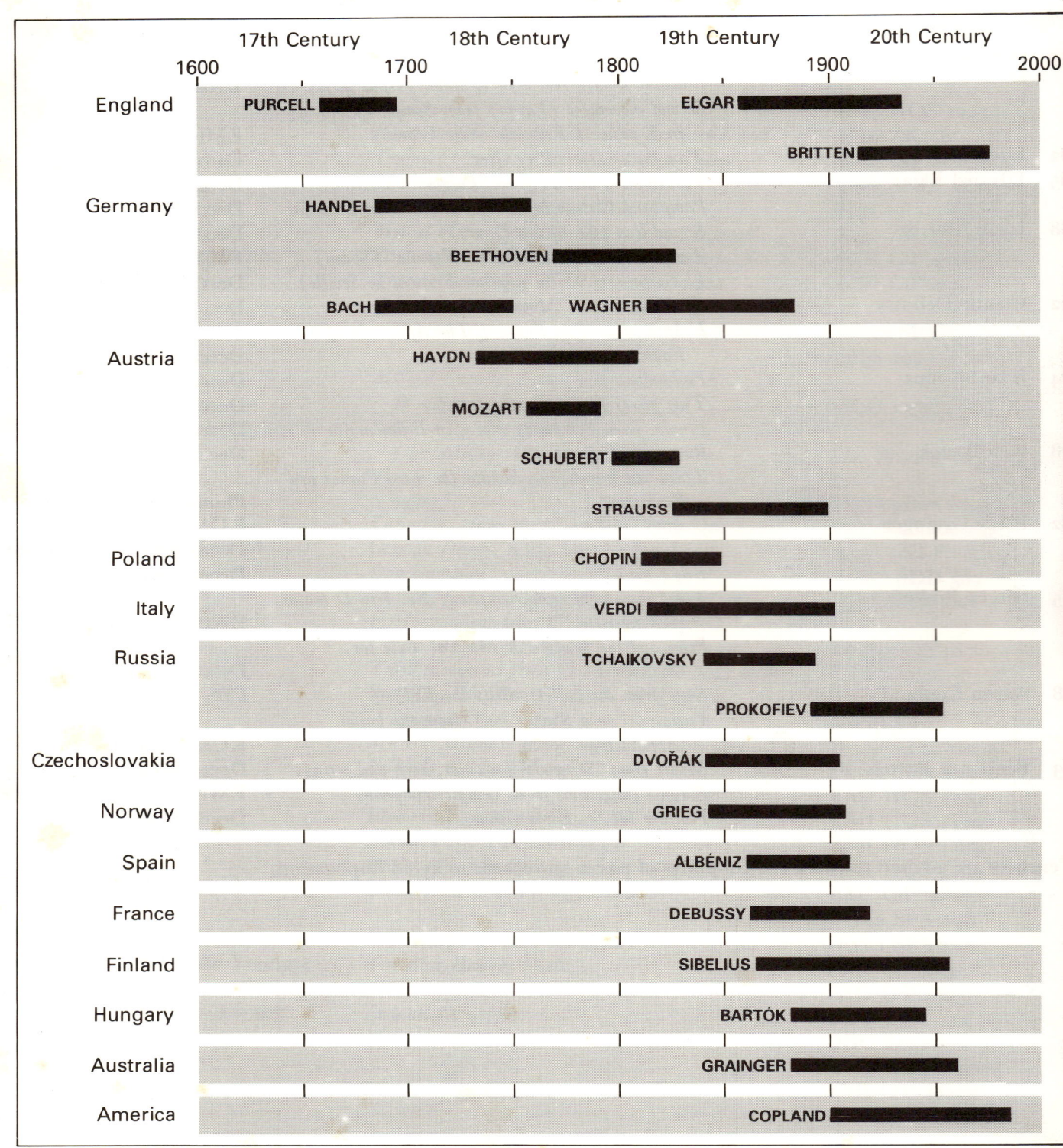

	17th Century	18th Century	19th Century	20th Century
	1600	1700	1800	1900	2000

England — PURCELL, ELGAR, BRITTEN

Germany — HANDEL, BEETHOVEN, BACH, WAGNER

Austria — HAYDN, MOZART, SCHUBERT, STRAUSS

Poland — CHOPIN

Italy — VERDI

Russia — TCHAIKOVSKY, PROKOFIEV

Czechoslovakia — DVOŘÁK

Norway — GRIEG

Spain — ALBÉNIZ

France — DEBUSSY

Finland — SIBELIUS

Hungary — BARTÓK

Australia — GRAINGER

America — COPLAND

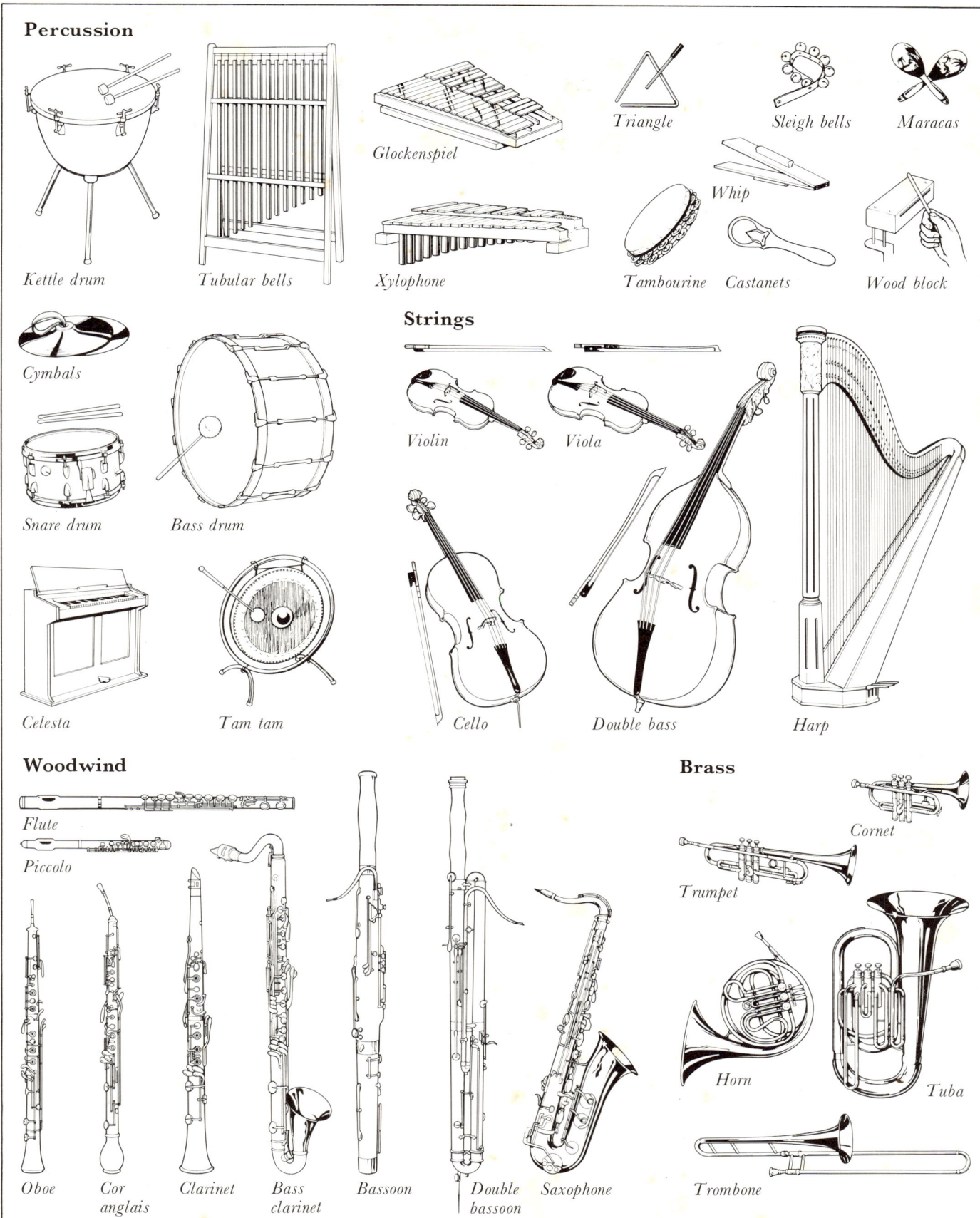

Percussion

Kettle drum

Tubular bells

Glockenspiel

Xylophone

Triangle

Sleigh bells

Maracas

Whip

Tambourine

Castanets

Wood block

Cymbals

Snare drum

Bass drum

Celesta

Tam tam

Strings

Violin

Viola

Cello

Double bass

Harp

Woodwind

Flute

Piccolo

Oboe

Cor anglais

Clarinet

Bass clarinet

Bassoon

Double bassoon

Saxophone

Brass

Cornet

Trumpet

Horn

Tuba

Trombone

TYLMAN SUSATO

died early 1560's FLANDERS (?)

There is quite a mystery surrounding the birth of Tylman Susato. It is not certain exactly where he was born – and no one knows when. But it was most probably at some time during the early 1500's.

In 1531 we find him mentioned as one of the five official trumpeters – the *Stadsspeelieden* of the city of Antwerp. And we also know that he worked in that city for several years as a composer and music-copyist.

A 16th century trumpeter

In 1551 Susato bought a piece of ground. On it he built his own printing works and a music shop which he called *In De Kromhoorn*, meaning

'At the Sign of the Crumhorn'. (You can find out what a crumhorn is on the next page.)

During the next few years, Susato published more than fifty music books containing, besides his own pieces, compositions by several other 16th century composers.

Music composed and printed by Susato

It was in the year 1551 that Susato published *Het Derde Musyck Boexken* or 'Third Music Book'. This contains an assortment of 16th century dances. Some of these, Susato based on true dance-tunes. Others are dance-arrangements which he made of well known songs, including a handful of the 'pop' songs of his day.

Susato does not mention which instruments are to play these dances. He leaves that for the performers to decide for themselves. He simply describes the music as 'pleasing and suitable to be played on all kinds of instruments'. However, a 'dance-band' of Susato's day would almost certainly have included all the instruments which are mentioned on the next page – and quite probably several others as well.

Recorders, of different sizes and pitches, were made of wood.

Viols had flat backs and sloping shoulders. The fingerboard was fretted (like a guitar's) showing where the fingers should go to find the different notes. The viol was held upright in front of the player, and the six strings were played with a bow.

The pear-shaped **lute** also had a fretted fingerboard, and its strings were plucked. The pegbox was bent back at an angle.

The **crumhorn** – which Susato chose for the sign outside his music shop – was a woodwind instrument. Its double reed vibrated inside a 'cap', giving a soft, very reedy sound.

The **cornett** was made of wood or ivory. It had finger holes like a recorder, but a mouthpiece like a trumpet.

The **sackbut**, made of brass, was the ancestor of the modern trombone, but the smaller 'bell' gave a more mellow sound.

Susato's dance band would probably also have included violins, harpsichord, regal (a small organ with reed pipes) and various percussion instruments such as tambourine, triangle, cymbals and tabor (a two-headed drum).

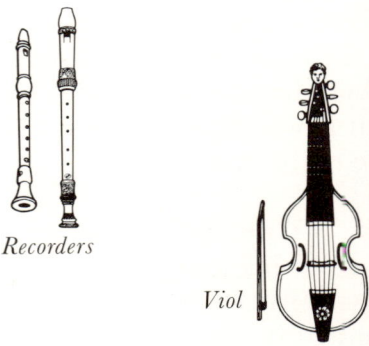

Recorders

Viol

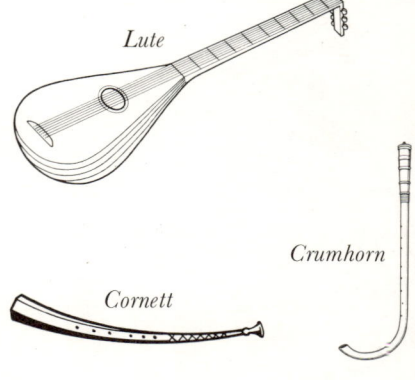

Lute

Crumhorn

Cornett

Sackbut

Two dances by Susato

Here are two dances from Susato's collection. The descriptions match the record by David Munrow – a brilliant young musician who died in 1976 – called 'Two Renaissance Dance Bands'.

Ronde
This lively 'circle-dance' is played by crumhorns, regal and sackbuts. It is built up from these three tunes:

Here is the order in which these three tunes are arranged:

A^1 A^2 A^3 A^4 B^1 B^2 A^5 A^6 B^3 B^4 C^1 C^2

A^1 and A^2 are played by a solo crumhorn above a drone (a long-held note) on the regal. We do not hear the sackbuts in every section of the dance. But when they do join in, their tone adds a rich fullness to the sound.

Pavane: 'La Bataille'

A *pavane* was a stately, strutting dance in which the couples advanced in a slow, majestic procession. In this particular pavane – whose name means 'The Battle' – it is possible that the couples formed two large groups which separated, turned, then advanced – like two armies joining in battle.

The music is in three sections. Tune **D** begins the first section. Listen for the rhythm which the tabor beats out from the beginning to the end of this dance.

In the second section, phrases played by the cornetts are solemnly answered by similar phrases on the sackbuts:

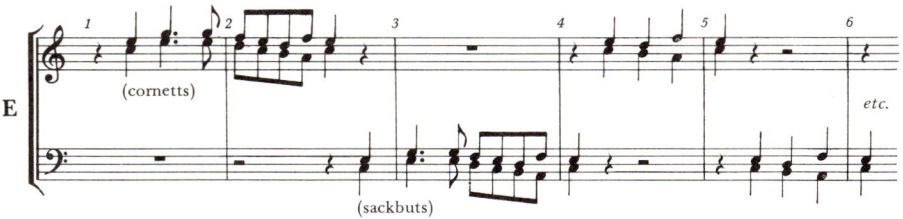

The third section is played by the full band. As the two opposing 'armies' slowly advance towards each other, the music builds up with fanfares in military style. The tabor still beats out its steady rhythm – now louder, and with exciting clashes on the cymbals.

HENRY PURCELL

1659–1695   ENGLAND

Henry Purcell

Henry Purcell is considered to be one of the greatest English composers. He came from a very musical family. His father and his uncle were both singers of the Chapel Royal. His brother Daniel also became a composer, and was very famous for his organ playing. And both his son and his grandson later became composers.

Purcell was born in London. We are not sure of the exact date, but it was probably during the year 1659. So as a boy, he lived through both the Great Plague (1665) and the Great Fire of London (1666).

At the age of eight or so, he was a singer of the Chapel Royal. When his voice broke, he left to become 'assistant keeper, maker, repairer, mender and tuner of the King's Instruments' – the King being Charles II. In 1677, he was appointed 'Composer in Ordinary to the Royal Household'. Two years later, he became organist at Westminster Abbey and, in 1682, of the Chapel Royal as well.

The music Purcell composed during his short but busy life is extremely varied. His official duties meant he had to provide music for many royal occasions – pieces for royal birthdays and funerals, and 'Welcome Songs' to celebrate the return to London after a royal journey. And as organist, he was expected to compose music for the church, such as anthems. But besides all this, he found time to write many songs and instrumental pieces and, in particular, a great deal of music for the theatre.

The beginning of a Sonata by Purcell

When he died, in 1695, Purcell was buried 'in a magnificent manner' in Westminster Abbey, close to the organ he had played during the last sixteen years of his life.

Hornpipe, from the Seventh Suite for harpsichord

Purcell's eight *Suites* (or 'groups of pieces') for harpsichord are mostly made up of dances. Originally, a 'hornpipe' was a single-reed woodwind instrument found in certain parts of the British Isles. It was used to provide music for a lively dance, chiefly associated with sailors. But later on, the name 'hornpipe' came to describe the dance itself.

Purcell's *Hornpipe* is built up in *binary* (or 'two-part') form. The music is in two sections, and each of these is repeated:

‖: **A** :‖: **B** :‖

The harpsichord

The strings of the harpsichord are plucked. When a key is pressed down, a strip of wood called a *jack* jumps up inside the harpsichord, and a *plectrum* plucks the string. Many harpsichords have two keyboards and two, or even more, complete sets of strings and jacks.

It is not possible to make the sounds on a harpsichord grow *gradually* louder or softer (as you can on a piano). But it is possible to vary them. Plectrums made of quill produce a bright, rich sound. Leather plectrums are softer and warmer sounding. Pulling out one of the 'stops' may allow two sets of strings to be played from one keyboard, making a louder, fuller sound. A 'lute stop' causes jacks to pluck nearer to the ends of strings, giving a softer, thinner tone.

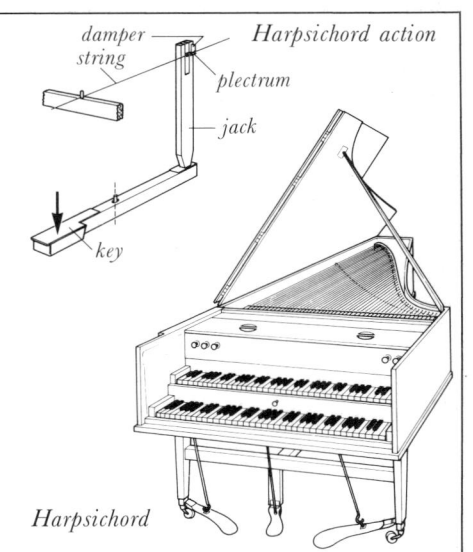

Harpsichord

Trumpet Overture, from 'The Indian Queen'

The Indian Queen was a play for which Purcell composed songs and orchestral pieces. The story of the play takes place in Mexico in the 16th century, and tells how Queen Zempoalla plots to snatch the throne from Montezuma, last Emperor of the Aztecs.

This *Trumpet Overture* introduces Act 3 of the play (*overture* means 'opening piece'). The music is in three contrasting sections:

1. A slow, very majestic introduction in a strong, rather jerky rhythm (Tune **A**, below).

2. The main, faster section of the Overture. Instruments enter in turn, playing Tune **B**:
   first violins – closely followed by
   second violins;
   violas;
   cellos and basses, with harpsichord;
   violins again;
   and finally, trumpet.
   Later on, listen for the first four notes of Tune **B** (marked in the bracket) to be tossed to and fro between trumpet and strings.

3. The Overture ends with slow, quiet music in which the trumpet is silent.

The trumpet

In Purcell's day, the trumpet had no valves and (like a bugle) could only play certain notes. A player had to find these notes by changing the pressure of his lips against the mouthpiece. The higher the note – the tighter his lips had to be.

It was not until early in the 19th century, when valves were invented, that other notes became possible. Now, on the modern trumpet, each of the three valves brings in an extra length of tubing – offering other whole series of notes. By using valves in different combinations, and also varying his lip pressure, a modern trumpet player can play any note throughout the range of his instrument.

Sometimes, for a different kind of sound, a trumpeter fits a *mute* into the bell of his trumpet.

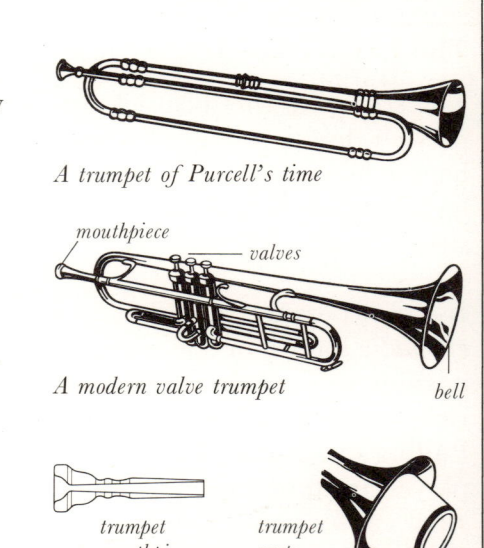

A trumpet of Purcell's time

mouthpiece
valves
A modern valve trumpet
bell

trumpet mouthpiece
trumpet mute

GEORGE FRIDERIC HANDEL

1685–1759 GERMANY (died in England)

Handel was born in 1685 (the same year as another great German composer, Bach), in Halle. His father intended that he should become a lawyer, but Handel became a violinist and harpsichord player at the opera house in Hamburg and, by the time he was twenty, had seen his first opera performed there.

He travelled to Italy – the leading musical country at that time – and stayed for five years, learning a great deal from the music he heard there. His own compositions, especially operas and church music, earned him high praise and when he returned home, he was recognised as a composer of brilliant talent.

In 1710, Handel visited England where he found Italian opera was all the rage. In just two weeks, he composed an opera called *Rinaldo*, which was performed with immediate success.

Returning to Germany, Handel took the post of *Kapellmeister* – or 'director of music' – at the court of the Elector of Hanover. After a year, he asked permission to visit England again, promising to return 'within a reasonable time'. But success and fame in London made life in Hanover seem very dull and unexciting. Handel decided to stay on – and in fact, remained in England for the rest of his life.

Then, in 1714, Queen Anne died. Her successor to the throne of England was none other than Handel's rightful employer, the Elector of Hanover, who now became King George I. This was rather embarrassing for Handel. He was now accepted as England's leading composer and so a meeting with the King could hardly be avoided.

At first, the King was angry at Handel's long absence from his court in Hanover. But he eventually forgave him. For a long time, it was believed that this came about on an occasion when the King and his court made a journey up the river Thames on the royal barge. Handel followed in another boat, filled with musicians playing pieces he had written which he called the *Water Music*.

The King, surprised and delighted by the music he heard echoing across the water, was said to have had Handel brought to him, and to have forgiven him there and then. But this is no longer held to be true. Handel did indeed compose the *Water Music* for a royal water-party on the Thames – but by then he had already regained favour with the King.

Suite: The Water Music

Handel's *Water Music* consists of twenty pieces altogether. You will often hear just a handful of these performed as a *suite* (or group of pieces) arranged by the conductor, Sir Hamilton Harty.

Allegro ('rather quickly')
In this piece, Handel contrasts different 'blocks' of sound, one against another. First we hear horns alternating with the rest of the orchestra; then woodwind alternating with strings:

You can imagine the splendid effect of this music by Handel – especially the horn calls – echoing distantly across the water from his boat of musicians.

A musical water-party on the Thames, painted by Zoffany

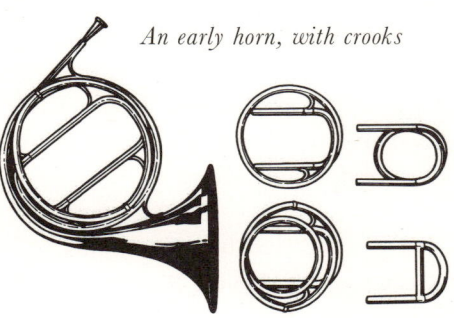

The early horn

An early horn, with crooks

Until valves were invented, the horn (like the early trumpet) could play only those notes available from a single length of brass tubing. A player could alter the total length by changing *crooks*. These were extra bits of tubing, graded in size. But although a different crook provided a new *range* of notes, the actual *number* available was exactly the same.

Here are three more pieces from Handel's *Water Music*:

Bourrée
A fast, crisp dance-tune with two main beats in each bar:

Hornpipe
Another lively dance, this time with three fast beats to a bar:

Allegro deciso ('rather quickly, and decisively')
Handel builds up this piece in what is called *ternary* form. *Ternary* means 'three', and so the music is arranged in three sections. The first and third sections are made from the same music (**A**). The second section (Music **B**) presents a contrast of some kind in the middle – making a kind of 'musical sandwich':

Here are the two tunes, **A** and **B**, used by Handel in this piece:

Music **A** soon brings in the exciting sounds of horns, trumpets and drums. Music **B** presents a contrast, and is for strings and woodwind only. Then Music **A** returns to end the piece.

Hallelujah Chorus, from 'Messiah'

Handel's *Messiah* is an *oratorio*. In an oratorio, the composer sets religious words (usually from the Bible) for choir and solo singers, accompanied by an orchestra. Unlike an opera, there are no costumes or scenery. An oratorio is not acted – it is just sung.

Of the many oratorios which Handel composed, *Messiah* is the most famous. It is a very long work, taking a whole evening to perform – yet Handel completed it in the amazingly short time of only twenty-four days. King George II was present at the first London performance of *Messiah* which took place in 1743.

The best-known piece from *Messiah* is the *Hallelujah Chorus*. (*Hallelujah* is a Hebrew word meaning 'Praise be to God'.)

The music begins with a short introduction for the orchestra; and then the choir bursts in, singing joyful 'Hallelujahs' (Music **A**).

Then follow the words: 'For the Lord God Omnipotent reigneth' (Music **B**). At this moment, the King was so impressed by Handel's music that he rose to his feet. This, of course, caused the entire audience to stand as well – so setting a tradition which is still followed to this day.

The final page of Handel's 'Messiah'; the crossings-out show how quickly he worked

The house in Lower Brook Street where Handel composed 'Messiah'

Arrival of the Queen of Sheba, from 'Solomon'

Solomon was one of the last oratorios which Handel composed, and this lively orchestral piece has been given this title since it begins Part 3 of the oratorio, when the Queen of Sheba arrives bringing gifts of gold, spices and precious stones to King Solomon.

Bustling strings announce the approach of the royal procession:

On several occasions during the music, Handel gives the two oboes fanfare-like solos to play:

The oboe

This woodwind instrument has a double reed – two pieces of cane, shaved at one end to a wafer thinness. When the player blows between them, the two reeds vibrate against each other, giving the oboe its characteristic, 'reedy' tone.

The oboe can sound sad in slow, smooth melodies; but perky and biting if given a fast, rhythmic tune to play.

The cor anglais, or English horn, is really a large kind of oboe with a deeper voice.

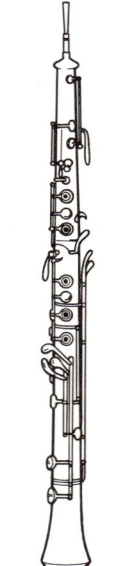

Handel conducting an oratorio

Not long after Handel had composed *Messiah* his eyesight began to fail. At the bottom of a page of one of his compositions we read: 'prevented from proceeding on account of the weakness of my left eye'.

In spite of several operations, Handel became totally blind. He continued to compose, however, relying on his secretary and music copyist, Christopher Smith, to write down the notes for him.

Handel died on April 14th, 1759. He was buried in Westminster Abbey, and it was said that three thousand people attended his funeral service.

George Frideric Handel

JOHANN SEBASTIAN BACH

1685–1750 GERMANY

Bach belonged to the largest and most amazing family in the history of music. We know of at least seventy-eight Bachs who were well-known musicians in their day. Bach himself married twice, and his two wives between them gave him twenty children – several of whom became composers or performers.

Bach was born in 1685 (the same year as Handel) at Eisenach in Germany. Both his parents died when he was nine years old, and so he went to live with an elder brother who was an organist. Bach used to creep downstairs secretly at night and copy out his brother's music by moonlight. One night, he was discovered. The music was locked away, but the boy kept his interest in music and learned to play the organ.

Unlike Handel, who travelled a great deal, Bach never left Germany, so he did not become truly famous during his lifetime. But he did move from town to town – sometimes taking a post as church organist, sometimes becoming director of music at the court of a rich nobleman. The last move he made was to the city of Leipzig where he became Cantor (organist and choirmaster) at St. Thomas's Church. Here, he was not only expected to train the musicians and compose all kinds of pieces for the church services, but to teach the choirboys their normal lessons as well.

Towards the end of his life, Bach – like Handel – suffered from failing eyesight. A gruesome operation was attempted. But tragically, this cost him what little sight he had left.

You will often hear it said that Bach's music contains a lot of 'counterpoint'. This means two, sometimes more, tunes weaving along all at the same time. So besides hearing a tune at the top, you will hear tunes going along in the bass and in the middle of the music as well.

First movement from Brandenburg Concerto No. 3 in G major

In a *concerto*, a soloist – or sometimes, a group of soloists – is given rather difficult music to play, accompanied by an orchestra. Bach composed six 'Brandenburg' Concertos. They are known by this name since Bach wrote them for a nobleman called the Margrave of Brandenburg. These concertos are now counted among Bach's greatest compositions – but it seems the Margrave himself did not think so. After he died, the music was found in his library in a dusty parcel, apparently never opened.

Each of Bach's six *Brandenburg Concertos* is for a different combination of instruments. Usually there is a small group of soloists contrasted against an orchestra of strings. In the *Third Brandenburg Concerto*, however, there is no *separate* group of soloists. This concerto is written for 3 violins, 3 violas, 3 cellos, a double bass, and harpsichord. Sometimes we hear all these instruments playing together. But all through the music, Bach selects first one combination of instruments, then another, to act as soloists, while the other instruments play an accompaniment in the background. And so different instruments are continually being chosen from the group – playing interesting solo passages for a moment or two, then making way for other soloists.

Bach's *Brandenburg Concerto No. 3* is made up of two 'movements', or separate pieces. Bach builds up the first movement almost entirely from this very rhythmic tune:

The opening snatch of this tune (with its very catchy rhythm: da-da-*dum* da-da-*dum*) is heard over and over again during this music. You will clearly hear this rhythmic snatch of tune passed around the orchestra – high on the violins, lower on the violas, lower still on the cellos and double bass.

This music is splendidly strong and vigorous. Listen to the contrasts which Bach introduces – in *pitch* (higher sounds against lower sounds); in *tone* – the firm, rugged tone of the bowed string instruments contrasted with the lighter, sparkling tone of the harpsichord; and above all, contrast between the sounds of a handful of players set against a much larger group.

String instruments

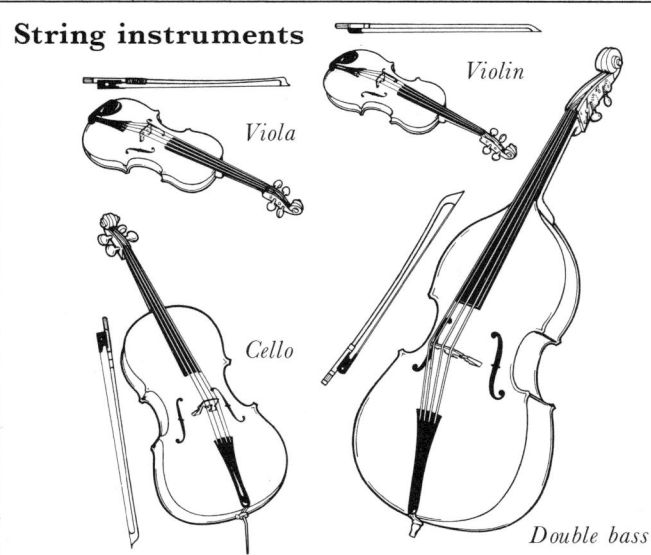

Viola

Violin

Cello

Double bass

The violin, viola, cello and double bass all make their sounds in exactly the same way. A bow (a wooden stick with horsehair stretched along it) is drawn across the strings to make them vibrate. Sometimes, the player plucks the strings with his fingertips. This is called *pizzicato*.

Violins, violas and cellos each have four strings. Double basses sometimes have five. On each instrument, the strings are tightly stretched across a 'bridge'.

To make the different notes, a string player must *shorten* the strings. He does this by pressing a string down with his finger. Only the length of string from his finger to the bridge can now vibrate. The shorter the length of string, the higher the note will sound.

The violin, the smallest of these string instruments plays the highest notes. The double bass plays the lowest, and is so tall that the player must either stand up, or perch upon a high stool.

Toccata and Fugue in D minor for organ

Bach wrote a vast amount of music of all kinds –
that is, except operas. During his lifetime,
however, he was known more as an organist
than as a composer. One of his most famous
organ pieces is the *Toccata and Fugue in D minor*.

The organ

On this page are pictures of two very different
kinds of organ. The first is more than 500
years old, and is being played in a home
rather than a church. As you can see, two
people are needed – one to play the keys,
another to work the bellows to pump air into
the organ. This organ has a single set of pipes,
graded in size – longer pipes for the lower
notes, shorter pipes for the higher ones. Each
key on the keyboard is connected to a pipe, so
when a key is pressed, air from the bellows is
allowed to go through the pipe, and a note is
sounded.

The second picture shows a large modern
church organ. As you can see, this is very
much more complicated. In modern organs,
the air is usually pumped by electricity. There
are two, three, or even more keyboards (called
manuals, from a word meaning 'hands'). And
there are many complete sets of pipes. Each
set produces its own special kind of sound.
One set may imitate a flute, another a
trumpet, and so on.

When *stops* are pulled out, whole sets of pipes
are connected to the keyboards. The organist
can mix together different kinds of sound, or
he can contrast one against another, playing
with each hand on a different manual.

The organist plays the lowest notes with the
pedals (from a word meaning 'feet'). The
pedals are made of wood, and are arranged in
a similar way to the black and white notes on
a keyboard. To play the pedals, the organist
uses the toe and heel of each foot.

Toccata comes from an Italian word meaning 'touch'. A toccata usually includes some brilliant, rapid fingerwork for the player, and is often very difficult music to play.

Bach's *Toccata in D minor* is a powerful and dramatic piece of music, full of strong contrasts. There are contrasts between loud and soft sounds, high and low sounds, between rapid running passages and long-held chords. Above all, there are contrasts between the many 'sound-colours' which the organ can provide – ranging from vivid, bright sounds to darker, richer sounds. This is how the *Toccata* begins:

The *Toccata* is followed by a *Fugue*, which is mainly built from this tune:

You will sometimes hear this fugue-tune played at a high pitch, sometimes lower, and sometimes very low indeed on the pedals.

In this *Fugue*, Bach also includes some 'echo-music' in which groups of notes are first played on one manual of the organ, and then echoed – with a change of sound – on another manual.

After the *Fugue*, Bach writes more music in the style of the opening *Toccata* to round off the whole piece.

Bach's *Toccata and Fugue in D minor* is sometimes heard in a version for full orchestra by the conductor, Leopold Stokowski. He conducted a performance of his arrangement of the piece in Walt Disney's film, *Fantasia*.

Chorale: 'Jesu, Joy of Man's Desiring' (from Cantata 147)

Cantata is an Italian word, meaning 'sung'. Like an oratorio, a cantata is usually a setting of sacred words to be sung by solo singers and a choir, accompanied by an orchestra. A cantata often ends with a *chorale* – which is a German hymn-tune.

Bach's chorale *Jesu, Joy of Man's Desiring* begins with this flowing, winding melody, played by a solo oboe:

Oboe

Then the choir starts to sing the chorale-tune. This tune has eight phrases – and Bach spaces these out so that as the voices rest after each phrase, the oboe continues to weave its flowing melody.

Je - su, joy of man's de - sir - ing, Ho - ly wis - dom, Love—most bright,

Drawn by Thee, our souls as - pir - ing, Soar to un - cre - a - ted light.

Word of God our flesh—that fa - shioned, With the fire of life——im - pas - sioned.

Stri - ving still to truth un - known, Soar - ing, dy - ing, round Thy throne.

Bach's chorale *Jesu, Joy of Man's Desiring* is often heard in an arrangement for solo piano made by the pianist, Myra Hess.

A choir is made up of four kinds of voices. These are:

Women	Men
sopranos (high)	tenors (high)
altos (low)	basses (low)

Air and Gavotte, from Orchestral Suite No. 3 in D major

Suite comes from a French word meaning 'follow'. It is used to describe a group of pieces played one after another. Bach composed four *Suites* for orchestra. In his day, there was no fixed idea of exactly which instruments should make up an orchestra. So in each *Suite*, he chooses a different combination of instruments. Bach's *Third Orchestral Suite* is written for 2 oboes, 3 trumpets, kettle drums, strings and harpsichord. First in the *Suite* comes a very majestic *Overture* (or 'opening piece'). Then follow four shorter pieces: *Air, Gavotte, Bourrée* and *Gigue*.

Air (or 'Song')

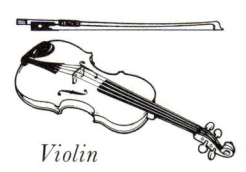

Violin

This is one of Bach's most famous pieces. It is for strings only, and the music is built up in two sections, each repeated. Beginning with a very long note, violins weave a curving melody which now rises, now falls. Beneath this melody, the lower string instruments tread softly in steady quavers:

Gavotte

A *gavotte* was a dignified dance, popular during the 17th and 18th centuries. It was moderate in speed, and had four beats to each bar. Each phrase began on the third beat of a bar.

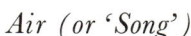

Trumpet

The *Gavotte* from Bach's *Third Orchestral Suite* is actually a *pair* of dances which are performed in this way:

Gavotte I	Gavotte II	Gavotte I

Here is the beginning of each of these dances:

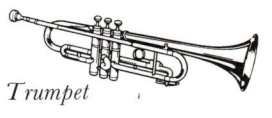

Oboe

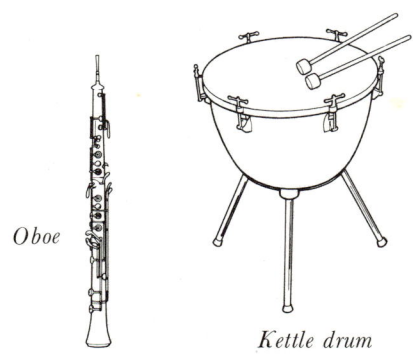

Kettle drum

JOSEPH HAYDN

1732–1809 AUSTRIA

Haydn was born the son of a wheelwright in the small village of Rohrau in Lower Austria. He was one of twelve children. The family was poor but musical, and in the evenings the children would often enjoy singing while their father accompanied them on the harp.

At eight years old, Haydn became a choirboy at St. Stephen's Cathedral in Vienna. When his voice broke, at seventeen, he was forced to leave the choir, and decided to rent a tiny attic in Vienna. For a time, he managed to earn his living by composing, playing and teaching.

When he was twenty-nine, Haydn was offered the post of *Kapellmeister* – or 'director of music' – to a rich Hungarian family named Esterházy. He now found himself in charge of an orchestra, choir, and many capable solo musicians. Each week, he was expected to compose, rehearse and conduct a vast amount of music – including orchestral and instrumental pieces for the palace concert room, operas for the Esterházy private theatre, and religious music for services in the

Josephus Haydn

The Esterházy Castle in Hungary

chapel. With so many capable musicians at hand, Haydn was able to try out new musical ideas and immediately judge their effect, altering and adjusting his music as he thought fit.

Haydn remained with the Esterházy family for thirty years. Then, when Prince Nicholas Esterházy died, he returned to Vienna. He continued to compose. He twice visited England, each time taking with him six symphonies for performance at concerts in London arranged by an impresario named Salomon. These, the last twelve of Haydn's 104 symphonies, are called the '*London*', or '*Salomon*', *Symphonies*. Haydn himself conducted them from the keyboard, as was the fashion at that time.

Haydn conducting from the keyboard

Second Movement from Symphony No. 100 in G (the 'Military' Symphony)

Haydn was one of the earliest composers to write symphonies. A symphony is a fairly lengthy work for full orchestra. It is usually made up of four separate pieces called 'movements', each one different in speed and mood.

This is how a composer of Haydn's time might plan out a symphony:

1st movement: fairly fast (but perhaps beginning with a slow introduction)
2nd movement: slower, and often song-like
3rd movement: a minuet and trio (the minuet was a popular 18th-century dance with three beats to a bar)
4th movement (*Finale*): at a fast pace

In Haydn's day, the only percussion instruments heard in symphonies were kettle drums (often called *timpani*). His *Symphony No. 100* was given the nickname 'Military' because it brings in extra percussion during the second and fourth movements. So as well as kettle drums, we hear triangle, cymbals and bass drum – instruments at that time associated with a military band rather than a symphony orchestra.

Besides percussion, the orchestra needed to perform Haydn's '*Military*' Symphony includes:

Strings	Woodwind	Brass
first violins	1 flute	2 horns
second violins	2 oboes	2 trumpets
violas	2 clarinets	
cellos	2 bassoons	
double basses		

Kettle drums (or timpani) are copper bowls with skin stretched tightly across the top. Tightening or slackening the skin raises or lowers the pitch of the note. The player can make single strokes, or he can play a 'roll' by using both sticks alternately and very quickly. Haydn used a pair of kettle drums in his orchestra. Nowadays there are three, or even more.

The **triangle** is a steel rod bent into the shape of a triangle but with one corner left open. The player can make separate 'tings', or play a *trill* by rattling the metal beater inside the top corner.

The big, **bass drum** gives out a low, booming noise rather than a clearly pitched note like the kettle drum. You may hear single 'booms', or a thunderous roll played with kettle drum sticks.

Cymbals are metal dishes which may be clashed against each other, or brushed gently together. A single suspended cymbal may be struck or rolled with drum sticks, hard or soft.

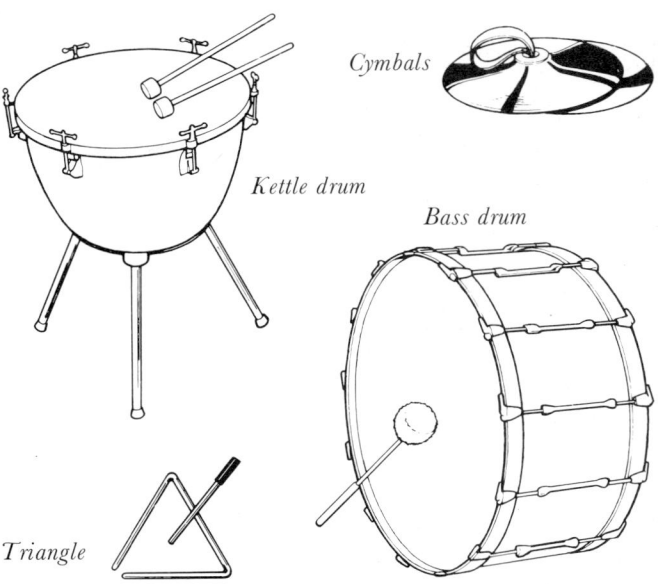

Cymbals

Kettle drum

Bass drum

Triangle

The second movement from Haydn's '*Military*' Symphony is built up in four sections. All four are based on this tune:

1. The first section is mainly for strings and woodwind. The tune is played first by violins and flute.
2. A sudden contrast! This second section uses the full orchestra, including the extra percussion instruments, and begins with the opening snatch of the tune (marked in the bracket), but played now in the *minor* key.
3. This section is very similar to the first – but makes more use of the full orchestra.
4. The movement ends with a *coda* (Italian for 'tail', or 'rounding-off'). It begins with a fanfare for the two trumpets.

'Gypsy' Rondo, from Piano Trio No. 25 in G major

This lively music was given this nickname because it has much of the flavour and high spirits found in Hungarian gypsy dances. *Trio* means 'three', and the three instruments you will hear in a piano trio are a piano, a violin, and a cello.

Haydn designs this piece in *rondo* form. In a rondo, the main tune keeps coming round, with other, contrasting, tunes heard in between. This is the main tune of Haydn's '*Gypsy*' Rondo:

Get to know this main tune first. Then listen for it as you hear a complete performance of this Rondo. How many times does the main tune come round?

Variations, from the 'Emperor' String Quartet

A *quartet* is music for four players, and the four instruments which play a string quartet are 2 violins, 1 viola and 1 cello. Like a symphony, a string quartet is usually made up of four separate movements.

Haydn composed more than 80 string quartets, of which the 'Emperor' is No. 77. It earned this nickname because, in the second movement, Haydn writes variations on a hymn tune he had once composed for the birthday of the Austrian Emperor. You may already know this tune. It was once the Austrian national anthem, but is now the national anthem of West Germany. And it is still often sung as a hymn tune to the words 'Glorious things of Thee are spoken'.

In this movement from Haydn's *'Emperor' String Quartet* we first hear this tune played by the first violin, while the second violin, viola and cello provide a hymn-like accompaniment.

Then Haydn writes four *variations* in which each instrument in the quartet plays the tune in turn. Haydn makes no alterations to the tune itself, but he disguises it each time by varying – or changing – the accompaniment in some new and interesting way.

This is what happens in each of the four variations:

Variation 1. The tune is now heard on the second violin against a running accompaniment in quicker notes, played by the first violin alone.

Variation 2. The cello takes over the tune. The second violin and the viola quietly accompany while the first violin weaves a descant, high above.

Variation 3. The tune passes to the viola. It is accompanied at first by the two violins, but later the cello joins in as well.

Variation 4. In this last variation, Haydn alters the harmonies, making the music sound more wistful. The tune is given to the first violin, soon soaring high above the other three instruments.

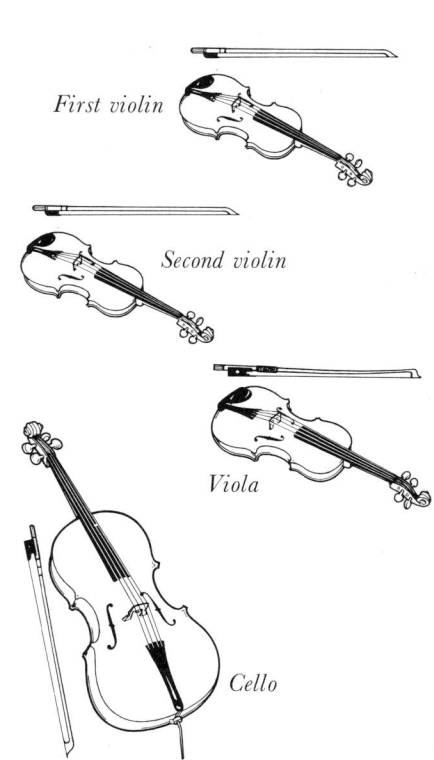

First violin

Second violin

Viola

Cello

WOLFGANG AMADEUS MOZART

1756–1791   AUSTRIA

The music of Mozart is probably loved and admired more than that of any other composer. He, of all composers, may truly be described as a musical genius. In his music, there is not only grace and beauty, but also the most perfect craftsmanship. It is said that Mozart could work out a piece of music, complete in every detail, entirely in his head. All that remained then was for him to set down the notes on paper. Mozart enjoyed ball games such as bowls or billiards, and it is very likely that he sometimes worked out compositions in this way while he was playing these games.

Mozart's brilliant musical gifts showed at a very early age. His father, Leopold, taught him to play the harpsichord when he was four. A year later, he was composing and playing his own pieces. Leopold took the young Wolfgang, together with his sister Nannerl, on long tours. The boy played at concerts, and before royalty, in most of the important cities of Europe. Everywhere, people were amazed at his musical abilities.

These were happy years. Later on, Mozart found life difficult, sometimes cruel. People took far less notice of the young man than they had of the brilliant child. For a great deal of his life, Mozart's genius was not truly appreciated, and several times he came very close to poverty. He was appointed director of music at the court of the Archbishop of Salzburg. But the Archbishop had little love of music and treated Mozart badly. When Mozart complained, the Archbishop actually had him kicked out of the room.

Eventually, Mozart settled in Vienna. At times, he had to teach to earn enough money to live. But it was here that he composed his finest music, including several of his 27 piano concertos, and his three last and greatest symphonies: *No. 39 in E flat*, *No. 40 in G minor*, and *No. 41 in C* (called 'The Jupiter'). Also, his three most important operas: *The Marriage of Figaro*, *Don Giovanni*, and *The Magic Flute*.

Yet in spite of the success of all these, and a great many other pieces, Mozart was still living in poor and miserable surroundings when he died – at the tragically early age of thirty-five. Few people bothered to attend his funeral, and to this day, no one even knows exactly where his grave lies.

To all Lovers of Sciences.

THE greatest Prodigy that Europe, or that even Human Nature has to boast of, is, without Contradiction, the little German Boy WOLFGANG MOZART; a Boy, Eight Years old, who has, and indeed very justly, raised the Admiration not only of the greatest Men, but also of the greatest Musicians in Europe. It is hard to say, whether his Execution upon the Harpsichord and his playing and singing at Sight, or his own Caprice, Fancy, and Compositions for all Instruments, are most astonishing. The Father of this Miracle, being obliged by Desire of several Ladies and Gentlemen to postpone, for a very short Time, his Departure from England, will give an Opportunity to hear this little Composer and his Sister, whose musical Knowledge wants not Apology. Performs every Day in the Week, from Twelve to Three o'Clock in the Great Room, at the Swan and Hoop, Cornhill. Admittance 2s. 6d. each Person.

The two Children will play also together with four Hands upon the same Harpsichord, and put upon it a Handkerchief, without seeing the Keys.

Announcement in a London newspaper, 1765

German Dance, K605 No. 3: 'Sleigh-ride'

Mozart composed several sets of dances for orchestra. Many of them are in the style of the Austrian dance called the *ländler* (pronounced 'lendler'). This was a peasant dance with three beats to a bar – rather like a waltz, but more heavy-footed. At first, the ländler was danced out-of-doors, but later it became a very fashionable dance in the ballrooms of Vienna.

Each of Mozart's *German Dances K605* is a ländler. The third, also known by the title *Sleigh-ride*, includes parts for 2 piccolos, sleigh-bells, and 2 posthorns – the long, straight, brass instruments which used to announce the arrival of mail coaches at towns or villages.

Mozart uses two main tunes in this music. Tune **A** begins on the full orchestra, and then is taken over by the 2 piccolos:

Tune **B** – accompanied by the sleigh-bells – has the rhythm and swing of a true ländler. The first part is shared by violins and bassoons. The second part is played by the posthorns.

Tune **A** is heard again. It is followed by a fanfare-like section of music which begins on the brass, then climbs higher in the violins.

Then we hear Tune **B** again with the sleigh-bells and posthorns – but Mozart now changes the ending of this tune.

Then he rounds off his music with a coda, in which the posthorns are accompanied by the exciting jingling of the sleigh-bells.

Sleigh bells

Posthorn

Piccolo

Don Giovanni

Mozart based his opera, *Don Giovanni*, on the old legend of Don Juan – a Spanish nobleman with a strong reputation for forcing his attentions on every pretty lady he meets.

The first scene is the courtyard of a palace in Seville. As the curtain rises, Don Giovanni is violently protesting his love for Donna Anna. He is suddenly interrupted by her father, the Commandant, who challenges Don Giovanni to a duel. They fight, and the Commandant is killed.

As the scene changes, Don Giovanni has already spied another lady. But this turns out to be Donna Elvira whom Don Giovanni once loved, but then deserted. He slips away while his servant, Leporello, reads her a list of Don Giovanni's many loves in countries all over the world:

'Here is Italy, six hundred and forty,
Next comes Germany, more than two hundred.
France and Turkey have each over ninety,
O but in Spain here, one thousand and three . . .'

Roaming the countryside, Don Giovanni comes upon a joyful group, celebrating the approaching wedding of two young peasants called Zerlina and Masetto. He orders Leporello to take everyone up to his castle – except, of course, Zerlina. When they are alone, Don Giovanni asks her to share her love with him:

(Don Giovanni)

You'll lay your hand in mine, dear, Soft-ly you'll whis-per 'yes';

'Tis not so far to go, dear, Your heart is mine, con-fess.

Zerlina What answer shall I make him? My heart will not be still;
I'd love to be a lady; surely he means no ill.

What is an opera?

An opera is a play set to music, acted and sung by solo singers (and often a chorus) accompanied by an orchestra. In some operas there are sections of spoken dialogue. But in others, every word is sung.

For the solo singers, there are *arias*, or 'songs', and you will sometimes hear the voices (perhaps accompanied only by a harpsichord) swiftly pattering off words in passages called *recitative*. The purpose of recitative is to 'tell the story'; arias are more tuneful and flowing.

Before the curtain rises on an opera, the orchestra plays an *overture*. This sets the mood, and often includes tunes to be heard later in the opera itself. Mozart's overture to *Don Giovanni* opens with rather menacing music, which returns towards the end of the opera when the stone statue of the dead Commandant visits Don Giovanni.

In the second act of the opera, Don Giovanni, escaping from yet another adventure, hides in a churchyard beside the huge stone statue of the dead Commandant. At the base of the statue, he reads: 'Here I wait till Heaven's vengeance falls on him who slew me'. Don Giovanni mockingly invites the statue to have supper with him. To his surprise, the statue answers: 'Yes!'.

Commandant slowly enters the room. 'Will you come with *me* to supper?' he asks. Don Giovanni mockingly accepts. He offers his hand to the statue who immediately seizes him in a firm, icy grip. He is given one chance to repent. But still he refuses. Flames burst up through the floor, and the voices of demons are heard as Don Giovanni is dragged down to hell.

The final scene shows Don Giovanni sitting alone at a banquet table. Donna Elvira rushes in and begs him to mend his ways. But he is unrepentant. As she leaves, she is heard screaming in terror. Leporello goes to see what is happening. He too cries out, then reappears and slams the door shut.

A loud knocking is heard. Don Giovanni takes a candle and opens the door himself. Suddenly all the lights go out, except the candle. In its flickering glow, the ghostly statue of the dead

The title rôle in *Don Giovanni* is sung by a baritone – a man whose voice lies midway between a bass (low) and a tenor (high).

Here are the characters in Mozart's opera, and the kind of voice which sings each part:

Don Giovanni	baritone
Leporello, his servant	bass
The Commandant	bass
Donna Anna, his daughter	soprano
Don Ottavio, her fiancé	tenor
Donna Elvira, a lady from Burgos	soprano
Zerlina, a country girl	soprano
Masetto, a peasant	bass

Minuet, from Symphony No. 39 in E flat major

At the time of Mozart and Haydn, the third movement of a symphony was a *minuet and trio*. A minuet was a graceful dance, with three beats to a bar, which had been very popular at the court of Louis XIV, the 'Sun King' of France.

Composers wrote minuets in pairs. The whole orchestra joined in the first minuet, but the second minuet was often played by three instruments only. And so composers called this minuet the *trio*, meaning 'three'. The minuet and trio were played in sandwich fashion, like this:

Minuet *(with repeats)*	Trio *(with repeats)*	Minuet *(without repeats)*

By Mozart's time, the speed of minuets had increased. The trio was no longer given to three instruments only – but its music is usually lighter in sound than that of the minuet, and there are often solos for wind instruments.

Here is the beginning of the *Minuet* from *Mozart's Symphony No. 39 in E flat major*:

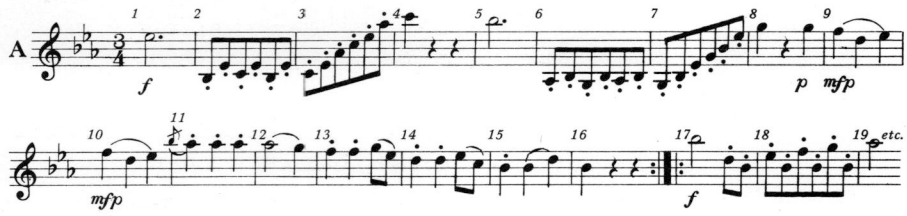

This is the beginning of the *Trio*, in which Mozart gives solos to two clarinets – one playing the tune, while the other plays an accompaniment in its lower, darker register:

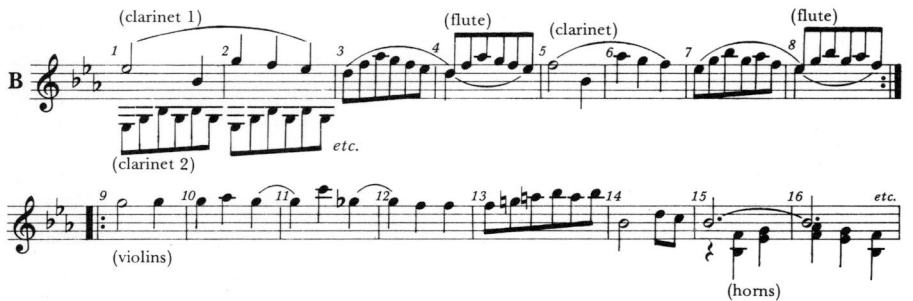

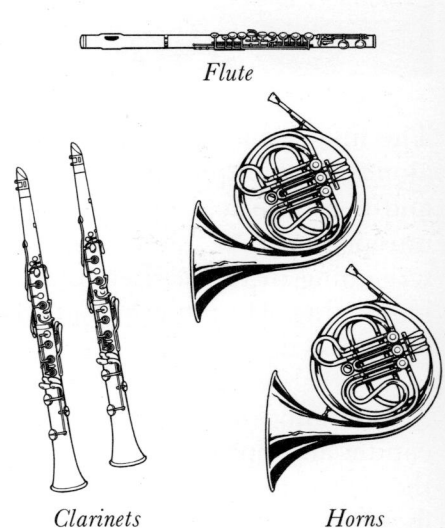

Flute

Clarinets

Horns

LUDWIG VAN BEETHOVEN

1770–1827 GERMANY

Beethoven's childhood was miserably unhappy. His father, who was a singer by profession, was determined that his son should swiftly become famous as a child musician. And so Beethoven was taught to play the piano and the violin from the age of four. He was severely beaten if he didn't practise enough. Sometimes his father would arrive home late from the tavern, very drunk. He would drag the boy from his bed and force him to practise at the piano.

Beethoven had his first composition published when he was eleven. At seventeen, he went to Vienna where he played to Mozart, who said: 'Watch this young man – he will make a great noise in the world!'. Later, for a short time, Beethoven took composition lessons from Haydn in Vienna.

Beethoven soon became famous in Vienna, both as pianist and composer. His music made a strong impact upon audiences. Listeners accustomed to the polished, 'polite' music of Haydn and Mozart found Beethoven's music often took them unawares. It appealed strongly to the emotions. And it was full of dramatic surprises – such as sudden contrasts between soft and very loud.

Whereas composing came very easily to Haydn and Mozart, Beethoven would struggle with a piece – crossing out, changing, improving it, until he was finally satisfied. He loved nature, and would take long walks in the country. He always carried a notebook in which he scribbled down any musical ideas which occurred to him. Later, tunes from these untidy pages would be altered time and again until he felt they were ready to be used. Beethoven became very careless of his appearance. During one of his country walks, he was arrested as a tramp and held by the police until his identity could be proved!

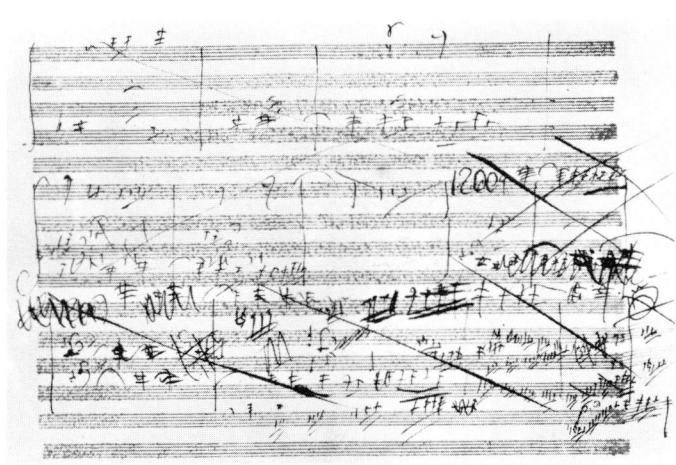

An untidy page from one of Beethoven's notebooks

Before he was thirty, Beethoven was horrified to realise that he was becoming deaf. At first, he desperately tried to believe this was just a passing illness. But it gradually grew worse and, eventually, he became totally deaf.

These are Beethoven's ear-trumpets, or hearing-aids

He had always been known for his rudeness and quick temper. Now, however, he quarrelled violently even with his closest friends. One day, a visitor found him pounding his piano in fury. Many of the strings had snapped due to Beethoven's desperate efforts to hear what he was composing. He was forced to give up playing and conducting at concerts. But Beethoven still continued to compose – now unable to hear his music except in his imagination.

First Movement from Piano Sonata No. 14 (the 'Moonlight' Sonata)

Beethoven composed 32 piano sonatas. A *sonata* is made up of three, sometimes four, separate pieces called 'movements'. Sonatas are usually for one or two instruments at the most – for instance, a piano; or perhaps a violin and piano.

Beethoven wrote the '*Moonlight*' *Sonata* in 1801. By that time, he already realised that he was becoming deaf. Most sonatas begin with a fairly quick movement, but Beethoven marks this first movement with the Italian word *adagio*, meaning 'slowly'. The title 'Moonlight' is not Beethoven's. The music took on this nickname when a critic said that this slow first movement made him think of moonlight shining on the Lake of Lucerne in Switzerland.

The music begins with gently rippling notes, smoothly grouped in threes. These soon become a hushed accompaniment to this melody:

This piano was presented to Beethoven by the London piano-maker, Thomas Broadwood

The violin

The violin has four strings. They are stretched across the bridge, and fixed to the tailpiece at one end and to the tuning pegs at the other.

To produce the sound, the violinist draws his bow across the strings. To make different notes, he must shorten the strings. He does this by pressing a string down against the finger board with his finger. The string can then only vibrate along the length from the bridge to the player's finger. The shorter the string, the higher the note will sound.

Instead of using the bow, the player may pluck the strings with his fingers. This is called *pizzicato*.

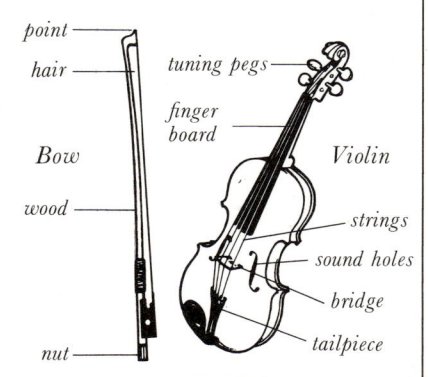

Third Movement from Violin Concerto in D major

In a *concerto*, a soloist (or sometimes, a group of soloists) is given rather difficult music to play, accompanied by an orchestra. A concerto is generally made up of three 'movements', or separate pieces:

1st movement: fairly fast
2nd movement: slower, and often song-like
3rd movement: swift, and usually light-hearted

Sometimes during a movement, the orchestra becomes silent while the soloist shows off his technique with some dazzling playing. A passage of music like this is called a *cadenza*.

The third movement of Beethoven's *Violin Concerto* is a lively *rondo*, in which the main tune comes round several times with different, contrasting, tunes played in between.

This is the main tune of Beethoven's Rondo:

You will also hear these two tunes which contrast with the main rondo tune:

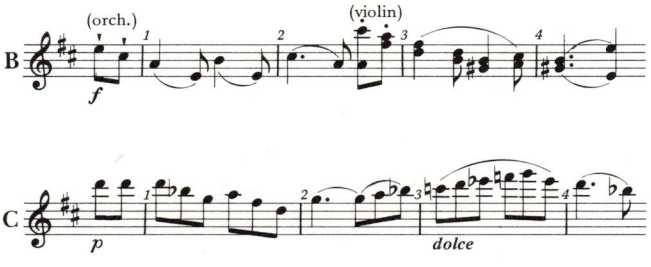

This plan of the Rondo from Beethoven's *Violin Concerto* shows the order in which you will hear the three tunes **A**, **B** and **C**:

A¹	B¹	A²	C	A³	B²	Cadenza	Coda
the main rondo tune	first contrasting tune	main rondo tune again	second contrasting tune	main rondo tune again	first contrasting tune again	(violin alone)	('rounding off') built on Tune A

Symphony No. 6 in F major (the 'Pastoral' Symphony)

This, the sixth of Beethoven's 9 symphonies, shows his great love for the countryside. Most symphonies are made up of four movements, but this one has five.

Beethoven's *'Pastoral' Symphony* is an example of what we call *programme music* – music which tells a story, or paints a picture in sound. Here, there is no actual story – but in each of the five movements, the music in some way describes the sights and sounds of the countryside as they might appear to someone more used to living in a town or city.

Beethoven gives each of his five movements a descriptive title.

First movement: 'Awakening of happy feelings upon arriving in the countryside'
The Symphony opens quietly with this tune, played by violins:

Later, there is a second, more flowing, tune:

Then Beethoven builds up the rest of this first movement mainly using these two tunes – or just fragments taken from them (for instance, the tiny scrap of Tune **A** marked in the bracket).

Peasants merry-making in a painting by the Flemish artist, Pieter Brueghel

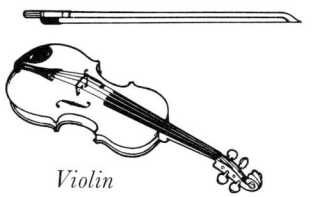
Violin

Second Movement: 'Scene by the Brook'
We know from one of Beethoven's notebooks that he actually spent quite some time beside a brook in the beautiful countryside not far from Vienna, jotting down ideas for this movement.

The music moves fairly slowly, but flows tunefully from the beginning to the end. Violins play the opening melody (**C**) while other instruments – two solo cellos in particular – suggest the peaceful rippling of the brook.

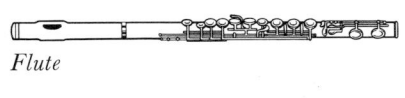
Flute

This movement of the Symphony is quite long. At the close, a flute, an oboe and two clarinets imitate the songs of a nightingale, a quail and a cuckoo.

Third Movement: 'Peasants' Merrymaking'
In this movement, Beethoven paints a musical picture of a group of peasants dancing and making merry after a hard day's work in the fields.

Strings begin a crisp, light introduction to this dance-tune:

Oboe

Clarinet

The second tune (**E**), beginning off-the-beat, is played by the oboe. Now and then, the bassoon joins in with just a few notes – sounding rather drowsy, as if from drinking too much wine!

The next section of music brings a sudden contrast: a louder, much more boisterous dance with two beats to each bar:

All these tunes come round again. Then we hear Tune **D** for the last time. The music grows louder and faster and rushes without a break into the fourth movement of the Symphony.

Fourth Movement: 'Thunderstorm'
A rumbling of distant thunder shudders on cellos
and double basses, and the pattering of the first
raindrops is heard on the violins:

Then the storm breaks with sudden fury. Brass
instruments and kettle drums add to the effect.
Jagged rhythms on violins and violas suggest
flashes of lightning, and rolls and crashes on
kettle drums imitate thunderclaps.

Eventually, the storm dies away. Woodwind
instruments paint blue skies, and the clear tone
of a solo flute leads the music straight into the
final movement of the Symphony.

*Fifth Movement: 'Shepherds' song. Happy and thankful
feelings after the storm'*
Beethoven designs this last movement as a
rondo, built upon this main tune – first hinted
at by clarinet and horn in turn, then played in
full by the violins:

This is how the famous French composer,
Hector Berlioz, described this final movement of
Beethoven's *'Pastoral'* Symphony:

'The Symphony ends with a hymn of
thanksgiving. Everything smiles. The shepherds
reappear, and answer each other on the
mountainside as they gather their scattered
flocks. The sky is serene. Calmness returns, and
we hear country songs and gentle melodies . . .'

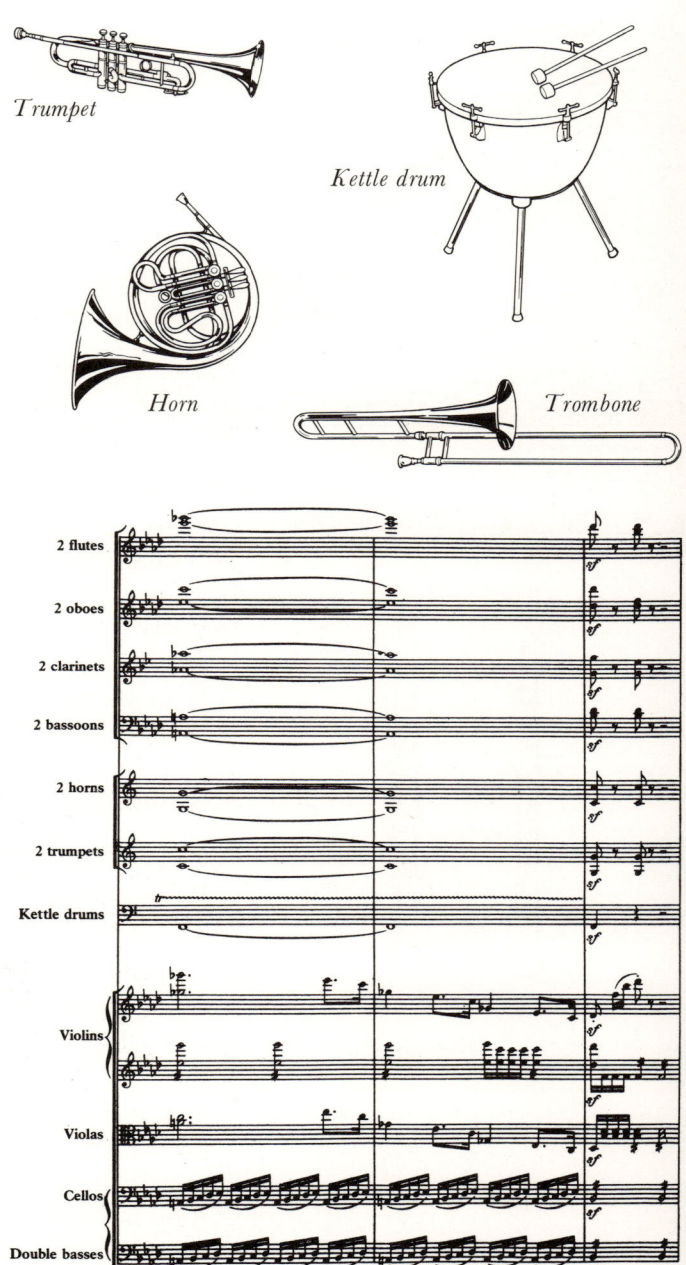

Above, you can see a page of the Storm music,
taken from the conductor's *orchestral score* – the
book containing the music played by all the
instruments. The instrumental 'parts' are printed
one below the other down the page, arranged
according to the four sections of the orchestra.

FRANZ SCHUBERT

1797–1828 AUSTRIA

Schubert was the son of a school teacher. He was born in Vienna, where he spent all his life. As a boy, he learned to play the piano and the violin, and had a beautiful singing voice. At the age of thirteen, he had composed several songs and piano pieces – but in secret, for he knew his father had strong ideas that he, too, should become a teacher.

When he was seventeen, Schubert joined his father at the school. He made a poor teacher however. His mind was usually on the music he was composing, instead of keeping order in the classroom. 'I was always annoyed by those children, who kept disturbing me!' he complained. He soon decided to give up teaching and to spend all his time composing.

Schubert died one year after Beethoven. He was only thirty-one. But during his brief life he composed a great deal of music of all kinds – more music, in fact, than many composers who lived twice as long. Schubert was always very poor (he would sometimes sell a song for only a few pence) yet he led a very happy life. He had many friends, and would often visit their houses to enjoy a musical evening, playing his piano pieces and accompanying singers in performances of his songs.

Marche Militaire in D major, for piano duet

Schubert wrote this Military March as a 'four-hand duet' – two people playing at one piano. In this music, the player sitting on the right takes the tunes, while the player on the left provides the accompaniment. Schubert himself must have taken part in many a performance of this piece at musical evenings shared with his friends. However, this brightly rhythmic and tuneful music became so popular that it is now heard in arrangements for all sorts of combinations of instruments, including full orchestra.

Schubert playing the piano in a performance of one of his songs

Schubert's *Marche Militaire* is designed in *ternary* form – three sections of music, built up from two main tunes, and arranged like this:

Section **A**	Section **B**	Section **A**

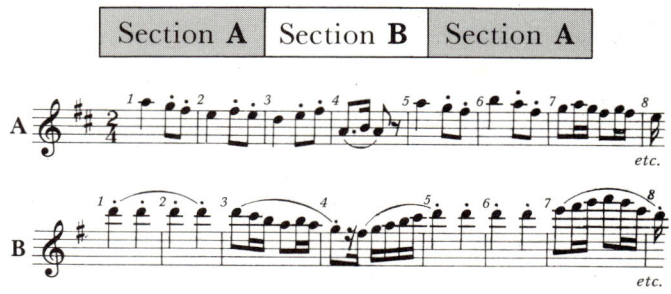

Erlkönig ('The Erlking')

Although Schubert composed a great deal of music of all kinds, he is best remembered by his songs. He wrote more than 600 songs (or *Lieder*, as they are called in German) and these touch on every possible mood and emotion.

Schubert composed his song called *The Erlking* when he was eighteen years old. It is a setting of a poem by the German poet, Goethe. One dark and very misty evening, Goethe heard the sound of galloping hooves approaching his house, Looking from his window, he glimpsed the dark figure of a horseman riding past at a desperate speed. The man was leaning forward, his arm cradled around a boy sitting in front of him on the horse. To Goethe, it seemed as if the boy were dead. Then swiftly, the horse and its two riders were swallowed up in the mist.

The poet, Goethe

This strange and rather frightening experience gave Goethe the idea for a poem which he called *The Erlking*. (On the opposite page, you can see how the poem turned out.) A few years later, Schubert set the poem to music. *The Erlking* became one of his greatest and most famous songs.

The courtyard of Schubert's house in Vienna

Schubert was one of the first composers to make the piano accompaniment in a song really important. The piano and the voice become equal partners. In *The Erlking*, the pianist's right hand plays thundering octaves and chords in groups of three from beginning to end, striking an atmosphere of terror, and perhaps suggesting the galloping of the horse's hooves. This piano accompaniment is extremely difficult to play.

The voice part, too, is fiendishly difficult. Not only must the singer become a narrator, telling the story, but he must also change his voice in different ways to present the three characters: the terrified boy, the father who is trying to comfort him, and the dreaded Erlking – the demon who haunts the forest through which they are riding.

Narrator: Who rides through the night when the wind is high?
A father clasping his child rides by.
His strong arm holds him secure from harm
And wraps him closely and keeps him warm.

Father: My boy, why cover your eyes with your hands?

Boy: The Erlking, father – look where he stands!
A crown he carries, a sweeping train;

Father: My boy, it's only the mist and rain.

Erlking: Come down with me, you handsome boy,
I've many a game and many a toy;
There's flow'rs to pick and there's fine clothes to wear,
And in all my mother has you may share.

Boy: But father, oh father, you hear what he sings,
You hear him telling of all the fine things?

Father: There, there boy! There is nothing to mind,
It's only the leaves that are tossed by the wind.

Erlking: Come down, pretty boy, come down and play
For here you may do as you like all day,
And after the revels that nightly they keep,
My maidens will rock you and sing you to sleep,
My maidens will rock you and sing you to sleep.

Boy: Oh! father, oh! father, I feel so afraid,
The Erlking's maidens are there in the shade.

Father: No, no! my boy, it's only the gleam
That shines on the willows down by the stream.

Erlking: You shall be mine, I'll seize you,
And should you resist,
My strength shall not spare you,
My will shall insist.

Boy: Oh! father, dear father, he won't let me go,
Erlking is hurting me, hurting so.

Narrator: The father shuddered, he spurred on amain.
He heard beside him a low moan of pain.
He reached his home in mortal dread,
In his arms – the boy was dead.

FRYDERYK CHOPIN

1810–1849   POLAND

Chopin's music quickly attracted attention. Besides performing at concerts, he was eagerly invited to play in the drawing-rooms of wealthy music-lovers. He made many friends – including the French painter, Delacroix, and the Hungarian composer and pianist, Franz Liszt.

Almost all Chopin's compositions are for piano alone. He received his first piano lessons from his sister at the age of four. He composed his first piece, a polonaise, when he was seven, and gave his first concert – playing a very difficult piano concerto – at the age of eight.

When he was twenty, Chopin left Poland – never to return. He took with him a small silver goblet filled with Polish earth, given to him by his friends. He travelled through Germany, giving concerts in several important cities. Then, a year later, he arrived in Paris. He was to make his home there for the rest of his life.

All his life, Chopin suffered from poor health. When he was twenty-eight, he became desperately ill with tuberculosis. He visited Majorca, hoping the climate there might improve his health. The inhabitants – afraid they too might catch the disease – demanded that he should leave the island. Instead, Chopin moved into a deserted monastery. Although he composed some of his finest pieces there, the chill and the dampness in the old building made his illness very much worse, and he was forced to return to Paris.

In 1848, Chopin visited England and Scotland. But loneliness – and the terror of knowing that he was dying – drove him back to Paris. He died there the following year. Earth from the silver goblet, brought with him from Poland eighteen years before, was sprinkled on his grave.

Polonaise No. 6 in A flat major, Opus 63

A *polonaise* is a Polish processional dance with three beats to a bar. The steps of a polonaise are very stately – almost 'walked' rather than danced. Yet the music itself is extremely rhythmic.

Although Chopin left Poland when he was twenty, never to return, his country was never far from his thoughts. In his Polonaises, he conjures up vivid musical pictures of the chivalry and pageantry of Poland's colourful history.

Chopin's *Polonaise in A flat major* begins with a dramatic introduction, which gradually builds up until it launches into this fiery main theme:

The mood of this music is proud and majestic. Now and then, the pianist plays a roaring scale passage which rushes angrily from almost the bottom to the top of the keyboard.

Later, listen for:
1. A brief tune (**B** below) which is accompanied by this typical polonaise rhythm:
2. The second appearance of the main theme (Tune **A**).
3. A section of music which begins with loud, spread chords. Then the left hand begins a rumbling *ostinato* (Italian for 'obstinately repeating'). Above this ostinato, rides Tune **C**.
4. The third, and last, appearance of Tune **A**, followed by an exciting *coda* to round off the piece.

Chopin often played this piano by the French maker, Erard

Etude in E major, Opus 10 No. 3

An *étude* is a 'study' – an often very difficult piece intended to improve a player's technique in some way. Chopin's 27 Etudes, however, are far more than just exercises for the pianist. 'Every one a poem!', wrote the German composer, Robert Schumann, when he first heard Chopin play them.

Chopin dedicated the first 12 of his Etudes to his friend, the famous Hungarian pianist and composer, Franz Liszt.

Chopin is often called 'the poet of the piano'. 'He really knows how to make the piano *sing*', wrote a critic – and this Etude begins with one of those smooth, singing melodies for which Chopin was so greatly admired (Tune **A**, below).

There is a change of mood in the middle section of the piece. The speed increases, and loud, pounding chords build up to a huge climax.

Then the tension relaxes, preparing the mood for the return of the peaceful opening melody.

Nocturne No. 2 in E flat major

A *nocturne* is a 'night-piece' – music whose mood matches ideas connected with night, such as calm, mystery and moonlight.

Chopin composed 21 Nocturnes. In these pieces, the pianist's left hand plays a smooth

accompaniment while, above, the right hand sings a flowing melody. (It was exactly this kind of piece which earned Chopin the title: 'poet of the piano'.)

Beneath the main melody of the *Nocturne in E flat*, Chopin adds the words *dolce espressivo* – 'sweetly and expressively'. We hear this melody several times. Each time it is repeated, Chopin decorates it in a slightly different way.

From time to time he brings in another tune – very similar in mood to the main melody:

Only towards the end of the piece does the music become rather more forceful and dramatic. Then, after high trickling notes played by the right hand alone, the Nocturne ends in the same hushed mood as it began.

Waltz No. 7 in C sharp minor

A *waltz* (sometimes called by its French name, *valse*) is a lilting dance with three beats to a bar. However, unlike the orchestral ballroom variety by composers such as Johann Strauss, Chopin intended his Waltzes to be played and listened to, rather than danced.

Each of Chopin's Waltzes is made up of several sections of music which are contrasted in mood and speed. The pianist's right hand is often given very difficult notes to play, while his left hand provides a simple waltz accompaniment.

Chopin's *Waltz in C sharp minor* has three tunes. Tune **A**, in the minor key, is melancholy in mood and moves at a gentle speed:

Tune **B**, also in the minor key, is made up of patterns of swift, darting quavers:

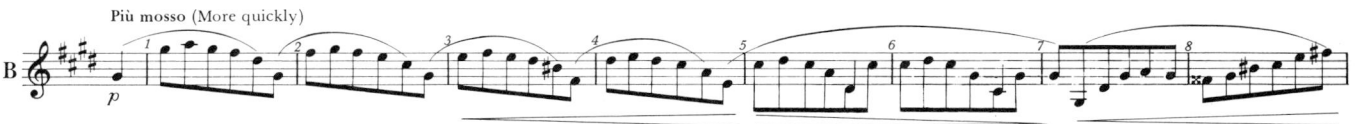

Tune **C** is in the major key, and is slower and more wistful:

Chopin arranges his three waltz-tunes in this order:

A   B   C   B   A   B

Several of Chopin's piano pieces (including the *Waltz in C sharp minor*) have been arranged for orchestra to provide music for the ballet *Les Sylphides* – 'The Sylphs'. (In mythology, a sylph is a spirit of the air.) The setting of *Les Sylphides* is a wooded glade by moonlight.

RICHARD WAGNER

1813–1883 GERMANY

Everything about Wagner's music is big, powerful and dramatic. His operas – or 'music-dramas' as he called them – are often very lengthy, and composed with a large stage in mind, with elaborate costumes and scenery. Wagner's singers require great acting skill, besides having powerful, tireless voices. The orchestra Wagner uses is often huge – with a particularly large brass section. This may include 8 horns, 4 trumpets, 4 trombones, and as many as 5 tubas.

Wagner does not use his orchestra simply to accompany the singers. In his operas, voices and orchestra are richly blended together in a continuous flood of sound which is made up of countless themes, called *leitmotifs*. Each of these themes represents a character taking part in the opera, or perhaps a particular mood or emotion, or even an object, such as a sword or a ring.

Wagner's best known operas are *The Flying Dutchman*, *Tannhäuser*, *Lohengrin*, *Tristan and Isolde*, *The Mastersingers* – and the four separate operas

making up *The Ring of the Nibelung*, intended to be performed on four successive evenings.

Overture, and Sailors' Chorus, from 'The Flying Dutchman'

Wagner was always borrowing vast sums of money from people, and so getting himself deeply into debt. In July 1839, he owed so much money to so many people that he thought it wisest to leave Germany in secret. He and his wife (together with their dog, called 'Robber') were forced to cross the border at night by way of a smugglers' path. There was a very serious risk of being shot by the frontier guards.

Eventually, they boarded a ship bound for England. The voyage should have taken eight days. Instead, due to terrifying storms and rough seas, it lasted more than three weeks. At one point, the ship was almost wrecked when it struck a reef. But in spite of these dangers, the journey gave Wagner the idea for a new opera: *The Flying Dutchman*.

Wagner based his opera upon an old legend. The mysterious Flying Dutchman is a sea captain, doomed, together with his crew, to sail the seas for ever. Once every seven years, however, he is allowed to go ashore for one day only. If he can find a girl who is willing to give up her life for him, the curse will be broken.

The opera tells how the Flying Dutchman meets Senta, the daughter of another sea captain. Senta has already seen a painting portraying the Flying Dutchman. She alone guesses who he really is, and longs to help him. They fall in love. But when the Dutchman discovers she is already promised to someone else, he prepares to sail away. As his ship leaves the bay, Senta runs up onto the cliffs – then throws herself into the sea. Immediately, the curse is broken.

Overture

The overture to Wagner's opera *The Flying Dutchman* is played before the curtain rises. The music uses tunes to be heard later during the opera. It not only sets the mood for the action which follows, but very briefly tells the story.

The overture begins with the desperate theme of the Flying Dutchman himself, played by the horns (Tune **A**). This is set against violent storm music. The lower strings play rising and falling scales, and there are thunderous rolls on the kettle drums.

The storm quietens and a gentler melody on the cor anglais introduces Senta (Tune **B**).

Afterwards, listen for snatches of each of these tunes, **A** and **B**, to be woven alternately against more storm music.

In the middle of the overture, Wagner brings in a tune used later in the opera as a sailors' chorus and dance. (You will find this tune printed at the bottom of this page.)

The overture ends with the same music which closes the whole opera – when Senta dies, and the Flying Dutchman is freed from the curse.

Sailors' Chorus

This vigorous chorus and dance opens the last act of the opera. Sailors of a Norwegian ship, moored alongside that of the Flying Dutchman, are making merry. They call to the sailors of the Dutch ship to join them – but there is only a weird silence.

Sailors are terrified by the appearance of the Flying Dutchman's ghostly ship

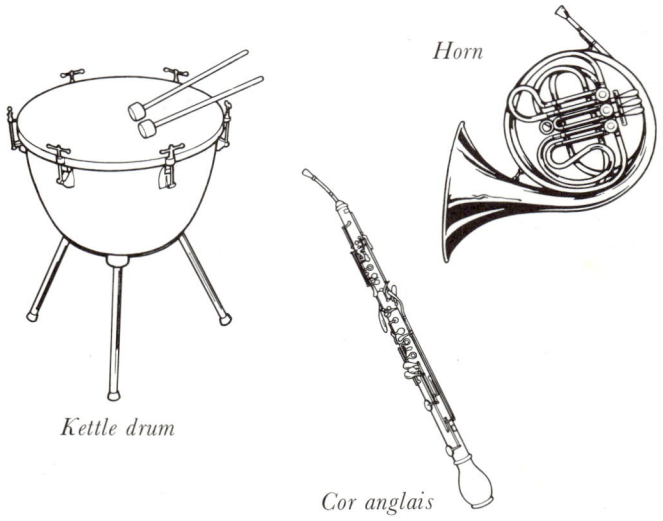

Horn

Kettle drum

Cor anglais

This is how the chorus begins:

Steers-man, leave___ your watch! Steers-man, leave___ your watch!

Ho,___ Hey,___ Ho,___Hey, Let the an-chor go! Furl the sails! Steers-man, here!

Prelude to Act 3 of the opera, 'Lohengrin'

Wagner's opera *Lohengrin* takes place in the 10th century. Gottfried, Duke of Brabant, has mysteriously disappeared. His sister, Elsa, is accused by Count Frederick and his wife Ortrud of murdering him. It is decided that Elsa must be tried according to Ordeal by Combat – her accuser shall fight any knight who is willing to defend her. But no knight steps forward.

Then a swan is seen gliding along the river, drawing a boat by a golden chain. In the boat stands a strange knight. Although no one knows it, this is Lohengrin, Knight of the Holy Grail. He tells Elsa he will champion her in the fight. If he wins, she will be his bride. But she must never ask his name, nor where he comes from. The combat is held, and Lohengrin is the victor.

The wedding of Elsa and Lohengrin takes place. Soon after, Count Frederick and his men attack Lohengrin. With a single blow, Lohengrin kills Frederick. He now tells everyone that he is Lohengrin, Knight of the Holy Grail which is kept in the temple at Montsalvat. As a Knight of the Grail, he is unconquerable – but only while his identity remains a secret. Having revealed it, he must now return to Montsalvat.

The swan is again seen drawing the boat along the river. Ortrud triumphantly claims that the swan is really Elsa's missing brother whom she had bewitched. Lohengrin, by his supernatural powers, restores Gottfried to his proper shape. The boat carries Lohengrin away down the river, now guided by a white dove of the Holy Grail.

Wagner divides his opera *Lohengrin* into three acts. The *Prelude* (or short overture) which begins Act 3 describes the joyful wedding festivities. The main tune is played first by horns; then by trombones and tuba:

The middle section of the *Prelude* consists of quieter music, featuring woodwind instruments. Then the vigorous main tune is heard again.

The trombone and the tuba

The trombone is the only instrument in the brass section of the orchestra which has no valves. Instead, it has a *slide* which the player slides in and out to alter the length of the tube. There are seven positions for the slide, each with its own range of notes which the player obtains by altering his lip pressure.

The tuba plays the lowest notes in the brass section. Its long tube, broadening into a wide 'bell', gives the tuba a rich, fat sound. Tubas may have three, or as many as five, valves.

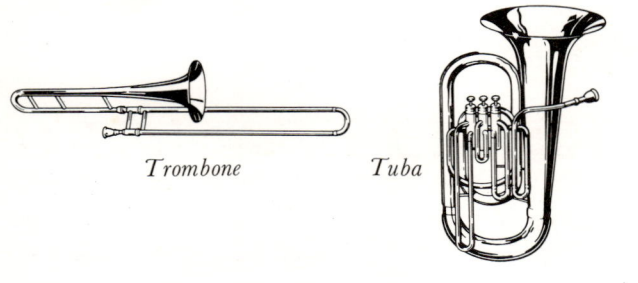

Trombone   *Tuba*

GIUSEPPE VERDI

Giuseppe Verdi is considered the greatest of all Italian opera composers. During his long life, he composed more than 30 operas, of which the best known are *Rigoletto*, *Il Trovatore*, *La Traviata*, and *Aida*.

Verdi was born the son of a village innkeeper, and even when he became world famous, he still remained a simple, honest peasant at heart. He bought a farm, spending as much time there as possible. He loved animals – especially dogs and horses. When away from home, he would send letters giving very detailed instructions about how they were to be fed and cared for.

Verdi had a flair for writing attractive tunes, and a sure instinct for building up vividly dramatic scenes in his operas. His characters are full-blooded, expressing their thoughts and feelings with powerful emotion. Verdi always considered the singers to be more important than the orchestra – but even so, he often supports the voices with exciting and strongly rhythmic orchestral accompaniments.

Il Trovatore (The Troubadour)

These are the main characters which take part in Verdi's opera, *Il Trovatore*:

The Count di Luna – a young nobleman of Aragon
Azucena – a gypsy woman
Manrico – the supposed son of Azucena, but really the brother of the Count
Leonora – lady-in-waiting to the Princess of Aragon

Act 1: The Duel

An important part of the story has already taken place before the opera begins. The Count di Luna's younger brother, as a baby, was said to have been cursed by an old gypsy woman. For this, she was burned as a witch. In revenge, her daughter, Azucena, stole the baby, intending to throw it into the same flames. But by a terrible mistake, she burned her own baby. She decided to bring up the stolen child as her son instead, calling him Manrico.

He, in fact, is the mysterious troubadour who has been serenading Leonora, lady-in-waiting to the Princess of Aragon. But the Count di Luna also loves Leonora – and challenges Manrico to a duel. (Both men are, of course, quite unaware that they are brothers.)

A dance in the gypsy camp

Act 2: The Gypsy

The scene is the gypsy camp on the mountainside. Dawn is
breaking. The gypsies begin to work at their forges, swinging
heavy hammers and crashing them down onto the anvils:

A See how the first ray of day-light re-turn-ing   B Who makes the gyp-sy's life of toil a life of plea-sure?

Manrico tells Azucena of his duel. How he disarmed the Count,
yet was somehow compelled to spare his life. Manrico learns that
Leonora, believing him dead, is about to become a nun.

The scene changes to a convent. The Count has come to seize
Leonora – but Manrico arrives in time to prevent him.

Act 3: The Gypsy's Son

The Count lays siege to the castle where Manrico has taken
Leonora. Soldiers capture Azucena as a spy. She is recognised as
the gypsy who threw the Count's brother into the flames. Azucena
denies this, but the Count holds her prisoner.

Manrico and Leonora are about to be married when news comes
that Azucena is to be put to death by burning. Already, the glow
of the flames can be seen from the window. As he leaves to rescue
Azucena, Manrico swears vengeance on all who would do her harm.

Act 4: The Execution

Manrico has failed to rescue Azucena. He has been captured and imprisoned in a tower where both he and Azucena now await death. Leonora arrives. She has a plan to save Manrico. A death bell begins to toll, and voices are heard chanting the *Miserere* – a prayer for the dying. Leonora is overcome with dread:

The pray'r for the dy - ing in sol-emn de-vo - tion! I hear it a-round me, it fills me with dread!

Manrico's voice is heard distantly from the tower, urging death to come quickly:

Oh, from this life of tor - ment why is there no re - lease?

The Count appears. Leonora offers herself to him if he will set Manrico free. The Count agrees. But Leonora has poison hidden beneath the jewel in her ring. As she enters the tower to tell Manrico he is free, she swallows the poison – then dies in his arms. The Count, in fury, orders Manrico to be taken out, then forces Azucena to watch his execution. As Manrico dies, Azucena points to the Count and shrieks: 'He was your brother!'. And then: 'Mother – you are avenged at last!'.

The soldiers capture Azucena as a spy

JOHANN STRAUSS THE YOUNGER

1825–1899 AUSTRIA

It is impossible to hear the name Strauss mentioned without thinking of Viennese dance music – especially the waltz, with its lilting, three-beats-to-a-bar rhythm.

Johann Strauss the Younger composed his first waltz when he was only six years old. His father – Johann the Elder, who was famous in Vienna as both composer and conductor – tried to discourage him from becoming a musician. But the boy took violin and composition lessons in secret and, at the age of nineteen, got together an orchestra of his own, playing music composed by his father and himself.

Five years later, when his father died, he joined their two orchestras together. He gave concerts throughout Europe and the United States, and was enthusiastically welcomed wherever he appeared as the leading composer and conductor of Viennese dance music.

The opening bars of 'The Blue Danube Waltz'

Johann Strauss the Younger composed almost 200 waltzes. Among them, are *Tales from the Vienna Woods*, which includes a haunting zither solo; *The Emperor Waltz*, beginning with two beats to a bar instead of three; and – most famous of all – *The Blue Danube*. Then there are other dances popular in Vienna at the time, such as mazurkas, galops and polkas.

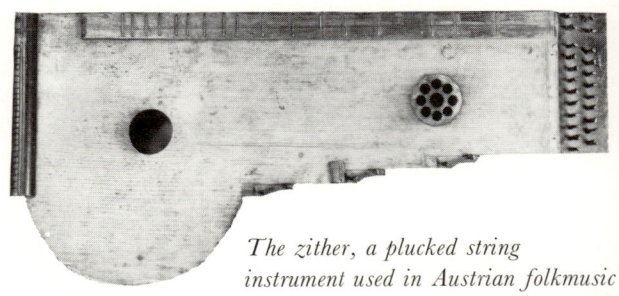

The zither, a plucked string instrument used in Austrian folkmusic

Johann also wrote several operettas (operas in a rather lighter style, in which the dialogue is spoken rather than sung). The best known of these is *Die Fledermaus* ('The Bat').

Each year, on New Year's Day, a special concert of music by the Strauss family takes place in Vienna. You may not be lucky enough to attend one of these concerts – but they are shown each year on television.

The Blue Danube Waltz

A waltz has three beats to a bar – usually in a *dum*-dah-dah kind of rhythm. When it was first danced in the elegant ballrooms of Vienna, at the end of the 18th century, a few people were shocked (the waltz was one of the first dances in which the partners held each other closely). But most people were captivated by the gaiety and lightness of its whirling movements and the 'waltz craze' soon swept right across Europe.

The Blue Danube must be the most famous waltz ever written. Like most waltzes by Strauss, this piece is really a whole *chain* of waltzes, each containing two tunes.

First, a slow, shimmering introduction in which horns mysteriously hint at the famous main theme (to be heard later as Tune **1A**). Then follows the chain of five contrasting dances with tunes that are joyful and lilting (**1A** and **3A**), broad and flowing (**4A**), and sometimes vigorous and strongly rhythmic (**5B**). Strauss's orchestration is varied and colourful – and you will often hear the snare drum bringing a crispness to the rhythms.

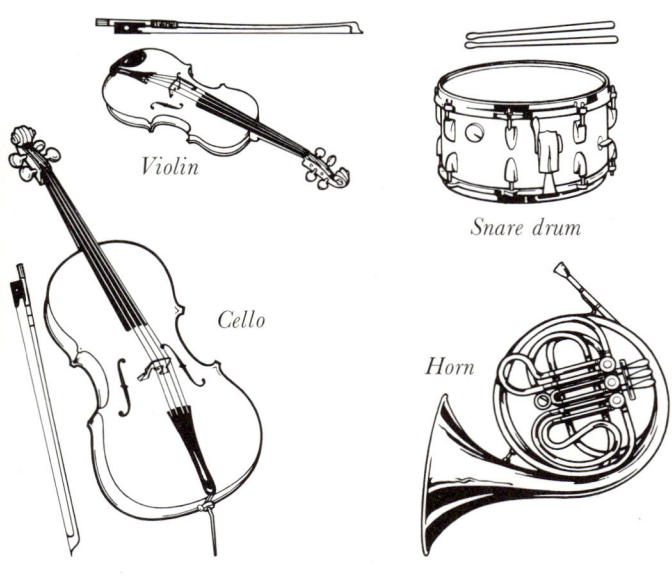

Violin

Snare drum

Cello

Horn

After the fifth waltz, Strauss reminds us of three of the tunes we have heard: **2A**, **4A** and **1A**. Then there is a sudden pause – followed by a *coda* (Italian for 'tail', or 'rounding-off'). This begins dreamily; but finally, the music sweeps to a breathless, whirling conclusion.

Here is a snatch of each of the ten tunes which make up this chain of five waltzes:

Pizzicato Polka

Johann Strauss the Younger had two brothers, Josef and Eduard, who also became composers. Johann and Josef both shared in composing this *Pizzicato Polka*. They gave it this title because, during the entire piece, the string instruments are played *pizzicato* (or plucked). Johann and Josef scored the music for strings alone – but it is sometimes heard in a version in which the strings are joined by woodwind and percussion instruments in the middle of the piece.

Pizzicato Polka is built up in three main sections. A plan of the music looks like this:

Section 1 **A B A**	Section 2 **C D**	Section 3 **A B A**	**Coda**

Notice that there are two tunes in each section but that the music of Section 3 is the same as that of Section 1. The piece is rounded off by a coda, during which the speed increases to make an exciting ending to the music.

These are the four tunes that you will hear:

The dance known as the polka was originally a folk dance from Czechoslovakia (or Bohemia, as it was then known). It takes its name from the Czech word *pulka*, meaning 'half', and the story goes that it was invented by a servant girl who was forced to take rather short steps as she made up the dance, due to the lack of space in her tiny attic room. Later, the polka was taken into the glittering ballrooms of Vienna, where it became almost as popular as the waltz.

Dancing in Vienna during the ball season

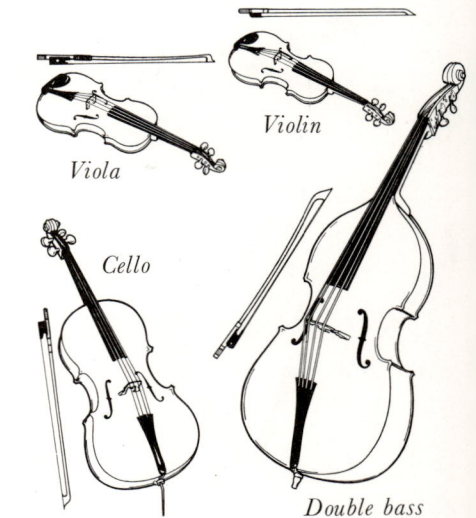

Violin

Viola

Cello

Double bass

PIOTR (PETER) IL'YICH TCHAIKOVSKY

1840–1893   RUSSIA

Tchaikovsky is one of the most popular of all composers. Few composers have written pieces which attract so many different kinds of people – even those who say they don't much care for 'Classical' music. His pieces appeal strongly to the emotions. They are full of superb tunes, and Tchaikovsky has a flair for using the orchestra in a vivid and exciting way.

Tchaikovsky was born in the Russian province of Vyatka. When he was ten, his family moved to St. Petersburg – the city now called Leningrad. Tchaikovsky was an extremely sensitive person, and suffered from nervous troubles all his life. He adored his mother, and was deeply affected by her death, from cholera, when he was fourteen.

It was decided that Tchaikovsky should study law, but also take music lessons at the same

time. When he was nineteen, he became a clerk in the Ministry of Justice. But four years later, he gave up his job to become a full-time musician.

Tchaikovsky's early compositions were not very successful. Even his *Fantasy-Overture: Romeo and Juliet* – one of his greatest pieces – was considered a failure at its first performance. Tchaikovsky found that in order to earn enough money, he had to spend more and more time teaching instead of composing.

In 1874, he began to compose his *First Piano Concerto*, dedicating it to Nicholas Rubinstein, director of the Conservatory of Music in Moscow. When Rubinstein tried it over, he made harsh criticisms and ended up by throwing the music on the floor, saying it was quite unplayable. Tchaikovsky, deeply wounded by Rubinstein's comments, tore up the dedication – fortunately not the music itself, which has become one of the best loved, most often played piano concertos ever composed.

Tchaikovsky's birthplace at Votkinsk

Tchaikovsky

In 1877, there came an important turning-point in Tchaikovsky's life. A wealthy widow named Madame Nadezhda von Meck, whose husband had made a fortune in building Russian railways, offered him a salary of six thousand roubles a year if he would give up teaching and spend all his time composing. There was one rather strange condition – that he should never try to meet her. Tchaikovsky agreed. But although they never met, many letters passed between them, describing in detail Tchaikovsky's thoughts and feelings about his music. This lasted for thirteen years. Then the payments, and the letters, suddenly ceased. Tchaikovsky never heard from Madame von Meck again.

Tchaikovsky was extremely self-critical, but easily became depressed when others criticised his music. When his last symphony, which he called 'The Pathétique', was received with little enthusiasm, he visited his brother in a state of deep depression. In his agitation, he took up a glass of unboiled water and drank deeply. During the evening, he became very feverish. A week later, it was announced that Tchaikovsky had died of cholera.

Tchaikovsky's work table

Andante Cantabile

This music is from Tchaikovsky's *First String Quartet*, but it is often played by a string orchestra. *Andante* means 'at a walking pace'; and *cantabile*, 'in a singing style'. In this piece, the string instruments are *muted* – a tiny comb is clipped onto the bridge, muffling the tone to make it sound hushed and silvery.

Mute

Two tunes are played alternately. Tune **A** is a Russian folk-song that Tchaikovsky heard one day sung by a carpenter working outside his room. Tune **B**, which is of Tchaikovsky's own invention, floats gently above a plucked *ostinato* – an Italian word meaning 'obstinately repeating'.

What is a ballet?

A ballet is a sequence of dances, usually telling a story – but no words are spoken. Instead, the story is told through the dancing and sometimes by means of hand gestures. Audiences quickly get to know these gestures, and so can follow 'conversations' which take place from time to time between the dancers.

Three of the world's greatest ballets were composed by Tchaikovsky. Their titles are *Swan Lake*, *The Sleeping Beauty* and *The Nutcracker*.

Music from the ballet: 'The Nutcracker'

The story on which Tchaikovsky based this ballet was called *The Nutcracker and the Mouse King*. The heroine is a young girl called Clara. As the curtain rises, an old-fashioned German Christmas party is about to begin. Clara's parents add the final decorations to the Christmas tree as guests begin to arrive. The candles are lighted and the children come forward to collect their presents. One of Clara's presents is a wooden nutcracker, carved and painted to look like a soldier.

When the party is over and Clara has gone to bed, she cannot sleep for thinking about her present. At midnight, she creeps downstairs. To her amazement, she finds a furious battle is taking place between an army of mice led by the Mouse King and an army of toys led by the Nutcracker. Just as the Nutcracker is about to be surrounded, Clara hurls her slipper at the Mouse King. The Nutcracker, whose life Clara has saved, immediately changes into a handsome Prince. He invites Clara to go with him to the Kingdom of Sweets, where the Sugar Plum Fairy is Queen. Arriving there, Clara is welcomed by the inhabitants as the heroine who has saved their Prince. She is entertained by special dances, performed in her honour.

Shortly after the first performance of *The Nutcracker*, Tchaikovsky collected together several of the pieces to make an orchestral *suite* which could be played at concerts. Here are five pieces from *The Nutcracker Suite*.

March
In the ballet, this music is played as the children march round the Christmas tree before receiving their presents.

The crisp first tune of the *March* is begun by trumpets, horns and clarinets, then taken over by violins. Every now and again, a cymbal is sharply struck with a kettle drum stick.

The short middle section of the *March* is a scurrying tune, played alternately by woodwind and violins. Then the first section of the *March* is played again.

Dance of the Sugar Plum Fairy

Tchaikovsky gives the melody in this dance to the celesta – an instrument, quite new at that time, which he had heard in Paris. The celesta is really a glockenspiel with a keyboard like a small piano. As keys are pressed down, tiny hammers strike steel bars to make a delicate, silvery, chiming sound.

The Sugar Plum Fairy

The celesta's melody is accompanied by *pizzicato* (plucked) strings, and the dark, rich sound of the bass clarinet:

Later on in the piece, the celesta is given a solo – light, rippling chords which climb higher and higher.

Trepak

A *trepak* is a fast, exciting Russian dance. At one point, the dancers vigorously kick out their legs from a squatting position.

Tchaikovsky includes the full orchestra in his *Trepak*. Much of the colour and excitement is provided by the tambourine.

The exciting ending of the 'Trepak'

Celesta

Bass clarinet

Chinese Dance

Two bassoons begin a crisp accompaniment which they will play right through this dance. They are helped by *pizzicato* cellos and double basses. High above, the tune is played first by a flute, then by shrill-voiced piccolos:

(flute)

(piccolos, one octave higher)

Afterwards, listen for bright, sparkling sounds from the glockenspiel. This percussion instrument (whose German name means 'play of bells') has metal bars, graded in size, which the player strikes with light mallets.

Dance of the Flutes

The first part of this dance is lightly and gracefully played by three flutes, above a *pizzicato* accompaniment for violas, cellos and double basses:

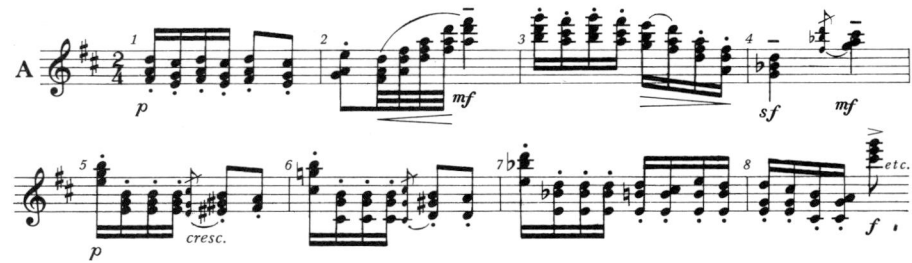

The middle part of the dance is a contrast, beginning with this music played by the full brass section – trumpets, horns, trombones and tuba – accompanied by kettle drums and cymbals:

Strings and woodwind join in. Then the lighter, more graceful music for the flutes returns to end the dance.

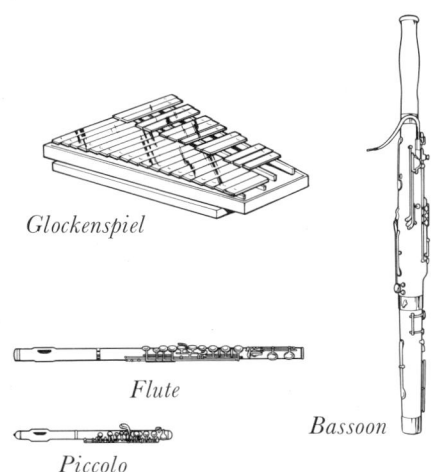

Glockenspiel

Flute

Piccolo

Bassoon

The flute and the piccolo

Although the flute belongs to the woodwind section, it is often made of metal. There is a hole in the instrument near one end. The player holds the flute horizontally and to the right, and blows across this hole – rather like blowing across the top of a bottle.

The lower notes of the flute are soft and full, but higher notes can be brilliantly clear.

The piccolo (its Italian name means 'tiny') is really a half-sized flute. It plays the highest and most brilliant sounds in the whole orchestra.

Scherzo, from Symphony No. 4 in F minor

Scherzo is an Italian word meaning 'a joke', and so a scherzo is usually a light-hearted piece. In the *Scherzo* from his *Fourth Symphony*, Tchaikovsky contrasts the sections of the orchestra. There are three tunes:

A is played by the string section only. No bows are used. Their music is entirely played *pizzicato* – plucking the strings with the fingertips.

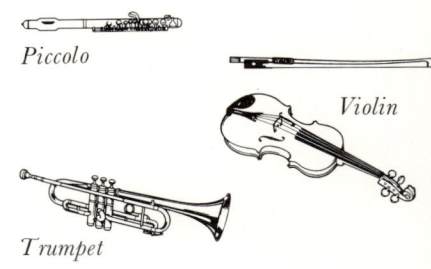
Piccolo

Violin

Trumpet

Kettle drum

B is given to the woodwind. The tune is played first by an oboe, then by a flute. Later, the shrill piccolo paints a bright ribbon of sound high above.

C suggests a military band passing by in the distance. This music is played by the brass with kettle drums marking the rhythm.

Soon, woodwind instruments join in the march, but playing their own tune (**B**) – first a clarinet, then the piccolo.

The strings return with tune **A**, played *pizzicato* as before. Then Tchaikovsky rounds off his *Scherzo* with an exciting *coda* in which all the orchestral sections join together.

Here is Tchaikovsky's plan for the music of this *Scherzo*:

Tchaikovsky's orchestra for this *Scherzo* includes:

Woodwind

1 piccolo	2 clarinets
2 flutes	2 bassoons
2 oboes	

Brass

4 horns	3 trombones
2 trumpets	

Percussion

kettle drums   (timpani)

Strings

first violins	cellos
second violins	double basses
violas	

A	**B**	**C**	**A**	**Coda**
strings only, *pizzicato*	woodwind only	brass and drums *(later, woodwind)*	strings only, *pizzicato*	all sections joining in

ANTONIN DVOŘÁK

1841–1904 CZECHOSLOVAKIA (BOHEMIA)

Dvořák's father was both the butcher and the innkeeper of a tiny village on the banks of the River Vltava. He was very fond of music, and often entertained visitors to his inn with a tune on the violin or the zither. So it was natural that his son should also take a keen interest in music.

At sixteen, Dvořák went to Prague to study music seriously. Later, he became a viola player in the orchestra of the newly-built National Theatre, where the conductor was the famous Czech composer, Smetana.

Eventually, Dvořák left the orchestra to become a full-time composer. He married, and settled down to a simple, contented way of life. He was a humble and very lovable kind of person. He cared deeply for his family, and was happy to compose in the kitchen of his home where the noises, instead of distracting him, seemed only to deepen his concentration.

Besides music and his family, Dvořák had three other loves. He was very fond of gardening, and he kept a large flock of pigeons. He also had a passion for trains! He would often stroll down to the nearby railway line to watch the huge engines roar past, and note down their numbers.

Humoreske in G flat major

A *humoreske* is a 'good-humoured' piece – usually very tuneful, and with a well-marked rhythm. Dvořák's *Humoreske* quickly became one of his best-known pieces. He composed it originally as a piano solo. However, when a composer writes a short piece like this which turns out to be very popular, the music is often taken up and arranged for other instruments to play. So you may hear Dvořák's *Humoreske* arranged for violin and piano by the famous violinist Kreisler, or perhaps in a version for orchestra.

Dvořák's *Humoreske* has three well-contrasted tunes, which are heard in this order:

Slavonic Dance No. 2 in E minor (Opus 46)

Dvořák composed two sets of *Slavonic Dances*, with eight dances in each set. He wrote all these dances first for piano duet – two people playing at one piano. Later on, the pieces proved to be so popular that Dvořák's publisher asked him to arrange them so that they could be played by a full orchestra. It was these *Slavonic Dances* which first made Dvořák famous throughout Europe.

All the tunes which Dvořák uses in his *Slavonic Dances* are of his own invention. But they all have the flavour of genuine Slavonic folk-melodies, and Dvořák bases each of the dances on the rhythms of an actual folk-dance.

Czech folkdancers in colourful costume

Dvořák's *Slavonic Dance No. 2 in E minor* is in the style of a *dumka*. This is a kind of Slavonic folk-ballad, whose music continually alternates between two sharply contrasting moods: darkly sorrowful, and wildly joyful.

Here are the two contrasting tunes which Dvořák presents alternately in this *Slavonic Dance*:

Tune **A** is in the minor key, and flows at a gentle speed. It is first played by the woodwind above *pizzicato* lower strings. Tune **B** is more rhythmic. This tune is in the major key, and is brisker and much more joyful.

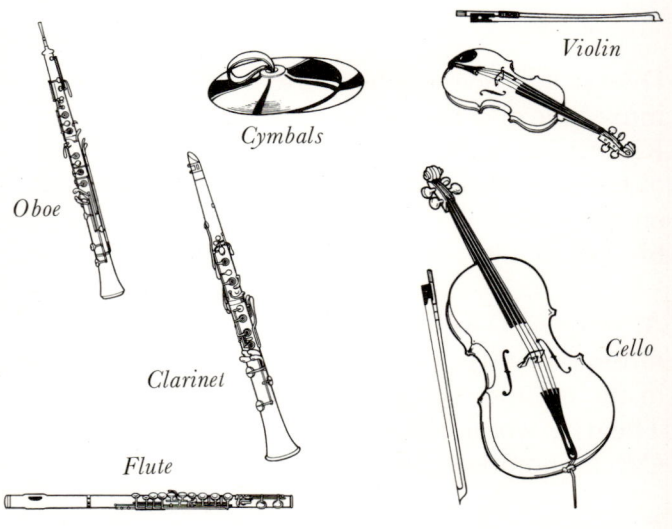

As you listen to this *Slavonic Dance*, notice that Dvořák rarely presents a tune in the same way twice over. As soon as a tune is repeated, he treats it in some new and interesting way. Sometimes he adds a 'counter-melody' – another melody played by different instruments, weaving along above or below the main tune.

Second Movement (Largo) from Symphony No. 9 in E minor ('From the New World')

After Dvořák had become world famous, he was invited to visit America. It was there that he composed the last of his nine symphonies, to which he gave the title 'From the New World'. While in America, Dvořák became fascinated by the huge liners which visited New York. He would often go down to the docks – especially if a famous ship was due. And he loved to be able to tell friends in Bohemia which ship would carry his letters to them. But in spite of the attractions which America offered, he became very homesick. These feelings seem to be reflected especially in the slow second movement of his *'New World' Symphony*.

The music begins with very soft, solemn chords for the brass. Then we hear a sad, quiet melody played by the cor anglais:

Later, listen for these three tunes:

Dvořák uses Tune **D** to build the music up to an exciting climax. While trumpets play a snatch of Tune **A**, trombones play the main tune from the *first* movement of the Symphony.

The music becomes calmer. The opening melody is heard once more (**A**), followed by the solemn brass chords which began the movement. Then the strings float softly upwards, and the music ends with mysterious-sounding chords for double basses only.

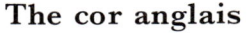

The cor anglais

The cor anglais (or English horn) is really a large kind of oboe, with a deeper voice. Its tone is dark, and rather melancholy.

61

EDVARD GRIEG

1843–1907 NORWAY

Grieg's mother was able to trace her family back to the Vikings. His father's ancestors had originally come from Scotland to settle in Norway after the Battle of Culloden in 1746.

Grieg took a keen interest in his country's folk music. In many of his pieces, he included Norwegian folk melodies or the rhythms of Norwegian folk dances. The freshness of his music appealed to many people, and he soon became known in other countries besides Norway.

Yet in spite of his fame, Grieg remained a shy man who liked nothing better than to live quietly at his house in the countryside near Bergen. He called his home Troldhaugen, which means 'Hill of the Trolls'. (A troll is a kind of dwarf, often found in Norwegian folk tales.)

In the grounds at Troldhaugen, Grieg built a hut – just large enough to take a piano, a chair and writing table, and a stove. Here, overlooking the beautiful Hardanger Fjord, he was able to write his music in complete peace.

Grieg's house, which he called 'Troldhaugen'

Two pieces from 'Peer Gynt'

In 1874, Norway's most famous playwright, Henrik Ibsen, decided to make a stage version of his long dramatic poem called *Peer Gynt*. He asked Grieg to compose some incidental music – pieces to introduce certain scenes, accompany some of the stage action, and to entertain the audience during scene-changes. Included in the music which Grieg composed for *Peer Gynt* are several of his best-loved pieces.

The hero of the play – Peer Gynt himself – is a selfish, headstrong, yet likeable character. Arriving uninvited at a wedding, he carries off the bride, Ingrid. For this, he is immediately branded as an outlaw – to be shot on sight.

Peer soon grows tired of Ingrid and leaves her. He decides to explore the caves deep beneath the mountains. This is the dark kingdom of the hideous trolls. They capture Peer and make him their prisoner, but fortunately he manages to escape.

Peer builds a hut for himself, high on the mountainside. Here, he is joined by Solveig, a girl from the village. Because of her love for Peer, she has left family and friends to be with him. But Peer, realising that he is not worthy of her love, decides to seek his fortune far away from Norway. He has many adventures but all his plans end in failure, and he is never able to find true happiness.

Eventually, an older if not wiser man, Peer decides to return home to Norway, experiencing storm and shipwreck on the way. When at last he arrives at the village where he was born, he finds that no one recognises him. No one even remembers the brave Peer Gynt.

He leaves the village and begins to climb the mountain. He meets a tall man, dressed all in black. As they talk, Peer realises it is the Devil in disguise. He has come to claim Peer's soul. In despair, Peer looks about him. He sees a hut, long forgotten on the mountain slope. The door opens – and Solveig, now old and blind, appears in the glow shed by the lamp. She recognises Peer's voice, and welcomes him with tears of joy. Peer's soul is saved – for the present – by the strength of her courage and her love.

Morning
This piece was really intended to introduce a scene showing Peer's adventures in North Africa. But Grieg's music sounds as cool and fresh as a spring morning in the mountains of Norway.

This melody is first played alternately by flute and oboe:

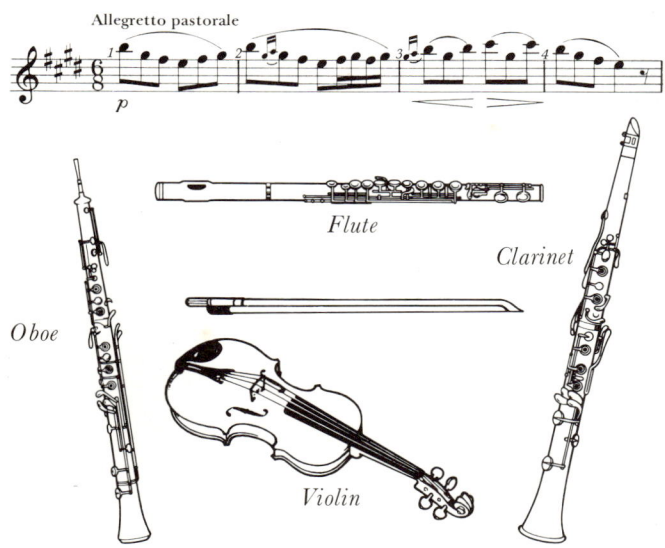

Flute

Clarinet

Oboe

Violin

Then we hear richer sounds from the strings – as if the rising sun suddenly bathes the landscape in its golden warmth.

Towards the end of the piece, woodwind instruments seem to suggest the songs of birds.

In the Hall of the Mountain King
This rather frightening, but exciting, music is
from the scene in the play when Peer explores
the dark caves beneath the mountains. This is
the kingdom of the hideous trolls and their ruler,
the Mountain King.

In the gloom, Peer becomes aware of shufflings
and scrabblings as weird shapes begin to creep
towards him from dark, shadowy corners. With
horror, he realises that he is being surrounded
by the trolls. Very slowly, they close in. . . .
Then suddenly, they attack – pinching, biting,
scratching. Desperately, Peer struggles to free
himself. But he is dragged forward, and thrown
down at the feet of the evil Mountain King. . . .

For this music, Grieg uses only one tune which
is played eighteen times. The piece begins very
softly and stealthily – and here, the bassoon
plays an important part. Then the music grows
gradually faster and louder, building up to a
terrifying climax.

Alla marcia (in march style)

The bassoon

This is the deepest-sounding
of the four main woodwind
instruments. Its tube is more
than 8 feet long, and so it is
folded back on itself to make
it more easy to manage.

The bassoon, like the oboe,
has a double reed. This is
fitted into the end of the
crook (given this name, as
you can see, because it looks
like a shepherd's crook).

The bassoon can sound
smooth and rather sad. But
when it is asked to play *staccato*
(making the notes sound crisp
and short), it can either
chortle along with good
humour or – as in this piece
by Grieg – sound gruff, and
perhaps menacing.

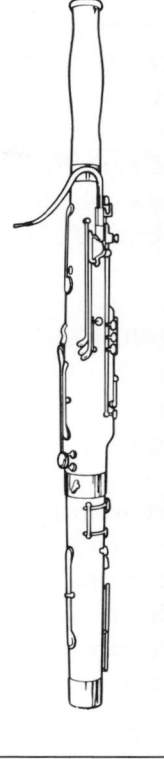

In the Hall of the evil Mountain King

EDWARD ELGAR

1857–1934   ENGLAND

Most composers study music at a college or university. Elgar taught himself – learning as he went along by playing and composing.

His father, besides being a church organist, kept a music shop in Worcester, and it was here that Elgar picked up a good deal of his musical knowledge. He taught himself to play several of the instruments in the shop, especially the violin and the bassoon. He became violinist in several small orchestras, and played bassoon in a local woodwind group. Sometimes he conducted as well. Many of his experiences at first hand, both as player and conductor, gave him a superb understanding of orchestration – the special technique of writing for full orchestra.

He began to compose in earnest, and had several orchestral and choral pieces performed, not only in Worcester, but in London as well. But it was not until the first performance of his *'Enigma' Variations* in 1899 that Elgar gained true recognition. People then began to realise that – for the first time for two centuries – England had a composer of worldwide importance.

The Malvern Hills

Variations 9 and 11 from 'Enigma' Variations

When a composer writes a set of variations, he takes a tune (which he calls the 'theme') and presents it over and over again, but always disguising it – or *varying* it – in different, interesting ways. He may take as his theme a tune that is already well known, or he may think up one of his own.

Elgar composed his *'Enigma' Variations* while he was living in Malvern. He dedicated the music 'to my friends pictured within'. And in fact, each variation is a musical portrait of one of these friends. Included are Elgar's wife, a pianist, a friend keen on amateur dramatics, a viola player, an architect (who built Elgar's house in Malvern), a music publisher, and an organist who owned a particularly lively bulldog. The last variation of all is a musical portrait of the composer himself.

Enigma means 'a puzzle', and the puzzle here is to do with the theme on which Elgar bases his variations. He mysteriously remarked that right through the music 'another, larger theme 'goes' – but is not played'. What this other, unheard tune actually is, no one has ever discovered, but many have tried to guess. (*God Save the Queen* and *Auld Lang Syne* have both been suggested.) However, this is the theme we *do* hear before the variations begin:

The theme is in *ternary* (three-part) form: **ABA**. **A** is played both times by violins, and is in a minor key. That, together with the effect of falling notes in each phrase, and a rest at the beginning of each bar, makes the music sound sad and hesitating. **B** presents a musical contrast. It is in the brighter-sounding major key, and is first given to woodwind instruments.

Variation 9 ('Nimrod')

Nimrod is the mighty hunter mentioned in the Bible. And this was Elgar's nickname for a friend of his, a music publisher named August Jaeger – the joke here being that in the German language, the word *jaeger* means 'a hunter'. This variation begins very softly on strings alone. Later, the music builds up to a huge climax – then, quite suddenly, dies away.

Elgar varies his original theme here by arranging it in three beats to a bar instead of four, and by putting it into the major key. But there is still a very strong likeness – match bars 1 to 4 of this variation against the same bars of the original theme.

Variation 11 ('G.R.S.')

These initials stand for George Robertson Sinclair, organist of Hereford Cathedral. But this music was really suggested by his bulldog, Dan, tumbling into the River Wye (bar 1), swimming earnestly for the bank (bars 2 and 3), then scrambling out with a joyful bark (bar 5). If you compare this music with the original theme, you will find that bars 2 and 3 are **A** in disguise. And that bar 4 is a very much quicker version of the first bar of **B**.

Pomp and Circumstance March No. 1 in D major

Elgar composed five marches which he called *Pomp and Circumstance*. When someone asked why an important composer should spend time writing marches, Elgar replied: 'I know that a lot of people like to celebrate events with music. To these people, I have given tunes.'

The most popular of these marches is the first. This brings in the tune to which the words 'Land of Hope and Glory' are often sung. Elgar became excited as he wrote this music, saying: 'I've got a tune that will knock 'em flat! A tune like that comes once in a lifetime.'

This is how Elgar builds up his march:
1. First a short, very fiery, introduction.
2. The first main tune (Tune **A**, below) is brisk and has a very lively rhythm.
3. The second tune (**B**) is broader, and more flowing. It is first played *piano* (softly) by the strings. Then *forte* (loudly), with brass and percussion instruments joining in.
4. The lively first tune returns.
5. The broad second tune (**B**) comes round again, with drums and cymbals to mark each beat.
6. Then Elgar brings his music to an exciting, sparkling conclusion.

Elgar's *Pomp and Circumstance March No. 1* is played at the last night of the Promenade Concerts in London each summer. Everyone joins in by singing these words:

'Land of Hope and Glory,
Mother of the free,
How shall we extol thee
Who are born of thee?
Wider still and wider
Shall thy bounds be set.
God who made thee mighty,
Make thee mightier yet!'

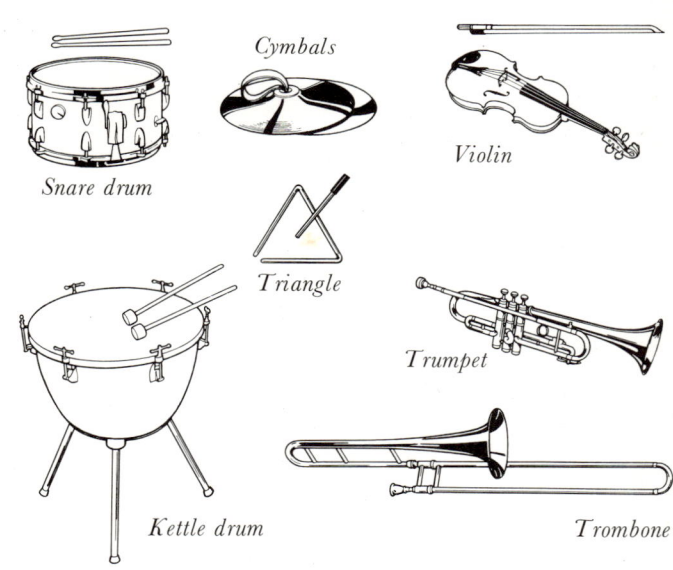

Snare drum

Cymbals

Violin

Triangle

Trumpet

Kettle drum

Trombone

ISAAC ALBÉNIZ

1860–1909 SPAIN

The early life of Isaac Albéniz reads like an incredible adventure story! As a pianist, he gave his first concert at the age of four. At seven, he played in Paris, and then took the entrance examination to become a student at the famous Conservatoire, or music college.

He played brilliantly, but amusing himself while waiting for the professors' decision, he sent a ball crashing through one of the Conservatoire's magnificent windows. He failed the examination – the official reason being that he was too young. So instead, he studied music in Madrid.

By now, he had begun to compose, and had heard a Spanish dance of his, called Paso Doblé, played by a military band in Barcelona.

When he was nine, Albéniz ran away from home, deciding to earn money from his piano playing. Apparently, one of his stunts at this time – which must have astounded his audiences – was to play sitting with his back to the piano!

Somehow, the boy managed to give concerts in several Spanish towns before a local mayor firmly put him on a train for home. But this did not suit him at all. He changed trains, went elsewhere, and gave more concerts. When robbers stole all the money he had earned, he simply made his mind up to earn more.

When he was twelve, Albéniz decided to try his luck abroad. He became a stowaway on board a liner bound for South America. He was discovered – but passengers and crew alike made a great fuss of him, and he was eventually allowed to land.

Incredibly, he gave concerts in Argentina, Uruguay, Brazil, Cuba, and Puerto Rico. Then he toured the United States from San Francisco to New York. At the age of fourteen, he decided to make for home – but stopped on the way to play at concerts in Liverpool and London.

Back in Europe, Albéniz took more piano lessons and composed a vast amount of music. Then, at eighteen, he achieved his greatest ambition – he went to Budapest to take lessons from the famous Hungarian pianist and composer, Franz Liszt.

Most of Albéniz's compositions are for piano. In many of them, we hear the rhythms of Spanish folk dances, and are often reminded of sounds of Spanish instruments such as the guitar and castanets.

Seguidillas (Castillian Dance)

Castille is a region of northern Spain. A *seguidillas* is really for both dancing and singing. Sung sections, called *coplas*, alternate with lively dance sections in a more definite rhythm. In a true *seguidillas*, guitar and castanets are used as an accompaniment.

Albéniz writes his piece for piano solo – but even so, in the dance sections there is a strong suggestion of the crisp clicking of castanets and the twang of guitar strings.

Castanets

A short introduction sets the rhythm going – then the dance begins:

This is the slightly slower tune of the *coplas*:

The countryside in Castille

A lively Spanish dance accompanied by guitar and castanets

69

Tango in D, from the Suite 'España' (Spain)

The modern ballroom dance known as the *tango* is Argentinian rather than Spanish – but originally, this dance came from the region of southern Spain called Andalusia.

A *tango* has two beats to a bar, and you will often hear this kind of rhythm:

Albéniz's *Tango in D* is the best known of all his compositions. Although he wrote this music for piano, it has been arranged for guitar by the great Spanish guitarist, Andrés Segovia.

Here is the rather wistful tune of Albéniz's *Tango*:

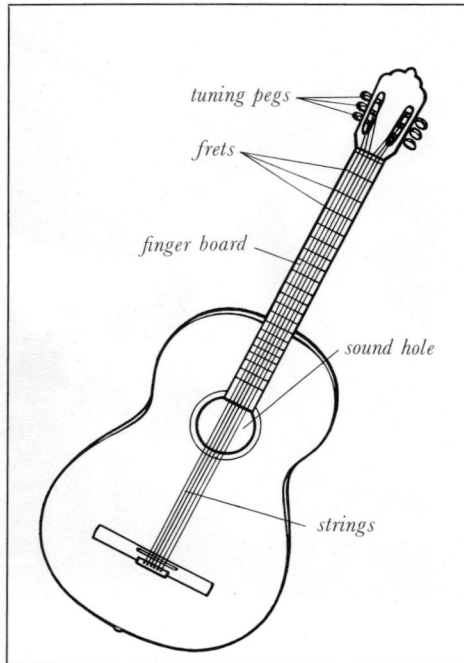

tuning pegs

frets

finger board

sound hole

strings

The guitar

The guitar is usually thought of as being a typically Spanish instrument – but nowadays, it is played in every country in the world. It is sometimes called the Spanish, or 'acoustic', guitar to distinguish it from the more modern electric guitar.

The six strings are stretched across a flat, hollow body, shaped like a figure 8. Each string is fixed to a tuning peg which can be tightened or slackened to adjust the pitch. The strings are plucked with the fingers of the right hand, or with a *plectrum* made of some kind of hard material.

On the fingerboard are thin strips of metal called *frets*. These show the player where to find the different notes by pressing down the strings with the fingers of the left hand.

The six strings are tuned to these notes:

El Corpus en Sevilla (Easter Festival in Seville)

This comes from a set of piano pieces which Albéniz called *Iberia*
– an old name for Spain. These pieces, which are considered to be
Albéniz's best work, present twelve musical pictures of different
parts of Spain. The style of piano-writing in these pieces reminds
us that, for a while, Albéniz took lessons from Liszt. All twelve
pieces are extremely difficult for the pianist – so difficult, in fact,
that Albéniz himself found them almost unplayable, and nearly
decided to burn them! The last piece in the set was completed in
the year in which Albéniz died. A few years later, a friend of his –
a Spanish conductor named Fernandez Arbós – arranged several
of the pieces for full orchestra. *El Corpus en Sevilla* paints a vivid
picture of an Easter Festival in the streets of Seville in southern
Spain.

This is how Albéniz builds up his music:
1. The crisp rhythm of a joyful march – quietly at first, as if a
   colourful procession is approaching from the distance:

Flute

2. The music becomes more flowing as a broad melody
   (**E**, below) is played loudly by the brass, above crashing drums
   and cymbals. Tubular bells suggest the triumphant pealing of
   all the church bells of Seville.

3. A slower, more peaceful section, in which the cor anglais (a
   large kind of oboe with a deeper voice) sings a melody which
   at first is very similar to Tune **E**.
4. The march music returns. It is interrupted by tune **E**, then
   continues on its way, gaining in speed and excitement.
5. The rhythm changes from two beats in a bar to three – and
   the march is transformed into a joyful, whirling dance.
6. A silence. Then the piece ends with slow, rather hushed music
   – as if night has fallen, and the festival is over.

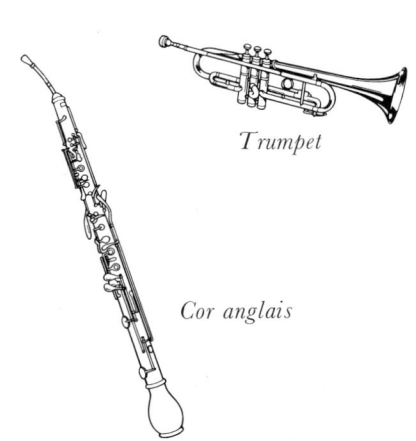

Trumpet

Cor anglais

CLAUDE DEBUSSY

1862–1918   FRANCE

Towards the end of the 19th century, French composers began to explore new paths in music. Their aim was to try to break away from writing music in the same style as previous composers – especially German composers who, for some time, had strongly influenced the music of other countries.

The most adventurous of these French composers was Claude Debussy. He experimented with mixing new combinations of instrumental tone-colours. He used chords in new and interesting ways, and based pieces on new, sometimes strange-sounding scales – such as the 'whole-tone' scale, which contains no

semitones but is built entirely from notes which are a whole tone apart:

Debussy's music is frequently compared with paintings by the group of artists known as the Impressionists. These painters did not try to make their paintings look 'real', as in a photograph. Instead, they painted merely an impression of what the eye might take in at a single glance – an impression of vague, hazy outlines, and the play of shimmering light and movement.

'Sunrise', by the Impressionist painter, Monet

Debussy often uses a similar 'impressionist' technique in his music – washes of shimmering sounds with bright splashes of instrumental colour. A good example of this is the beginning of the first piece from *La Mer* (The Sea) which has the title, *From Dawn to Midday on the Sea*. Here, as in all Debussy's music, light and shade, and especially mood and atmosphere, are very important.

Clair de Lune ('Moonlight'), from 'Suite Bergamasque' for piano

This is one of Debussy's most popular pieces. It is a musical impression of a calm, clear, moonlit night. This music requires the pianist to use a very delicate touch, and finely judged variations of light and shade. (Debussy once said that in many of his piano pieces, the player should try to imagine the piano as 'an instrument without hammers'.)

The music at the beginning of the piece is cool and silvery:

In the middle of the piece, the tone becomes warmer and richer as this melody floats above rippling notes for the left hand:

The harp

The harp has forty-seven strings, and seven pedals – one for each note of the scale. The pedals alter the tightness of the strings, so that each string can play any one of three notes.

Two typical harp sounds are *arpeggios* – spreading out the notes of a chord one after another; and the *glissando* – made by sweeping the fingers quickly across the strings.

L'Après-midi d'un Faune ('The Afternoon of a Faun')

In mythology, a faun is a creature of woodlands and forests – part human, but with pointed ears, and the horns, tail and feet of a goat. Debussy composed *L'Après-midi d'un Faune* after he read a poem by the French poet, Stephane Mallarmé. Debussy's music matches ideas in this poem, which describes a young faun lying beneath shady trees in the heat of a summer's afternoon. The faun spies a group of nymphs running through a cool glade. Are they real, he wonders? Or are they only in his imagination? His thoughts become hazier as he drowses in the heat.

Debussy's music magically suggests the mysterious, shadowy world of the faun, and the heat of the summer afternoon. This is how the music begins. The clear, warm tone of a solo flute plays a floating melody, followed by soft, distant horn calls accompanied by a glittering run on the harp:

JEAN SIBELIUS

Jean Sibelius [signature]

Finland lies between Sweden and Russia. About two-thirds of Finland is covered by forests of pine, spruce and birch. And everywhere, there are lakes. The Finns call their country *Suomi*, which means 'land of fens'. And it is sometimes called 'the land of sixty thousand lakes', as so much of the land is covered by water. In the north and east there are rivers, often with rapids.

Sibelius was born in the town of Tavastehus which lies about 48 kilometres to the north of Finland's capital city, Helsinki. He was christened Johan Julius Christian. Later, he took

the simpler name Jean, from an uncle who was a sailor. His father had wanted him to become a lawyer, but Sibelius tells how, after walking a whole day and a night in the forests, he made up his mind to become a composer.

Although he lived to be over ninety, Sibelius wrote most of his music before he was sixty. He composed mainly songs and orchestral pieces, including seven symphonies and several symphonic poems. A symphonic poem is music for orchestra which is descriptive in some way – perhaps telling a story, or painting a picture in sound. We often call this kind of music 'programme music'. Many of Sibelius's symphonic poems are based on *sagas*, or stories, from the *Kalevala*. This is the Finns' national collection of legends, telling of the adventures of gods and heroes from Finnish mythology.

Sibelius's music has been said to describe the sounds and rhythms of the Finnish countryside: sunlight on snow-covered pines, lonely lakes, forests at night, and icy winds sweeping across the Finnish landscape.

A Finnish landscape of lakes and pines

Finlandia

This is Sibelius's most famous piece. When he composed it in 1899, Finland was under Russian rule. The music aroused the Finns' feelings for their country so strongly that the Russians banned the piece. But Sibelius still conducted it at concerts under the disguised title of *Impromptu*. Finns look upon the broad hymn-like melody (**C**, below) as a second national anthem.

This is how Sibelius builds up the music of *Finlandia*:

1. A dark, menacing opening (Tune **A**) on snarling brass and kettle drums. This is followed by a smoother tune: first on woodwind, then strings.
2. Listen for loud trumpet calls, alternating with Tune **A** which is now played faster.
3. Rumbling kettle drums and double basses introduce the main section of the piece: again the trumpet calls – now with exciting cymbal clashes (Tune **B**). Then a rhythmic tune for strings with triangle.
4. The broad hymn-like melody is heard – first on the woodwind; then played right through again by the strings.

5. The trumpet calls are heard again, and the music grows to a huge climax with cymbal clashes off-the-beat. At the highest point, the kettle drums roar and the brass triumphantly reminds us of the hymn-like melody (**C**), now played much more slowly.

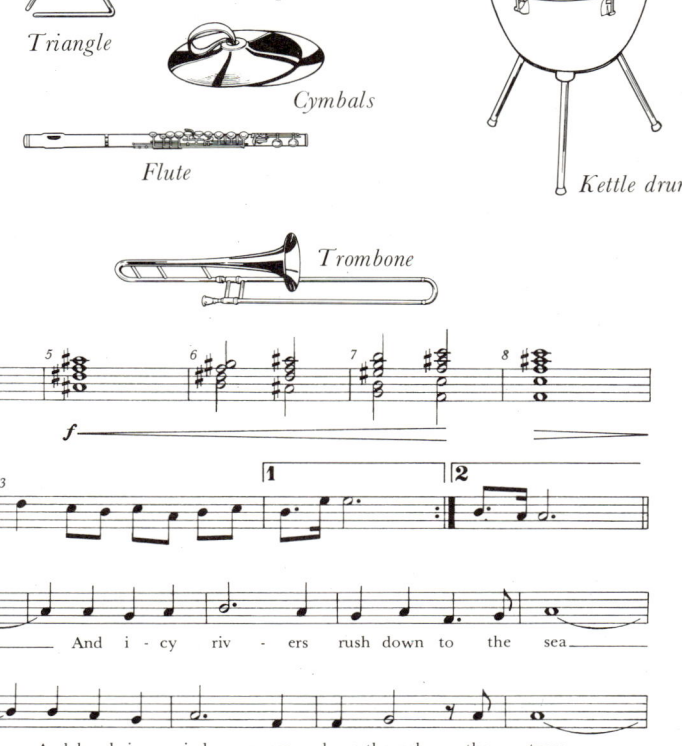

Triangle

Trumpet

Cymbals

Flute

Kettle drum

Trombone

A

B

C

This is my home where for-ests line the hill-sides,___ And i-cy riv-ers rush down to the sea

___ A-mid the snow where rein-deers roam the moun-tains_____ And howl-ing winds sweep down through the trees.

___ This is my land; These sounds of lakes and riv-ers_____ Will al-ways bring Fin-land-ia to me.

Two pieces from 'Karelia Suite'

When Sibelius composed this music in 1893, Karelia was a region of Finland lying next to the Russian border. After the Second World War, however, it became part of Russia. Sibelius composed these pieces to accompany a historical pageant about Karelia.

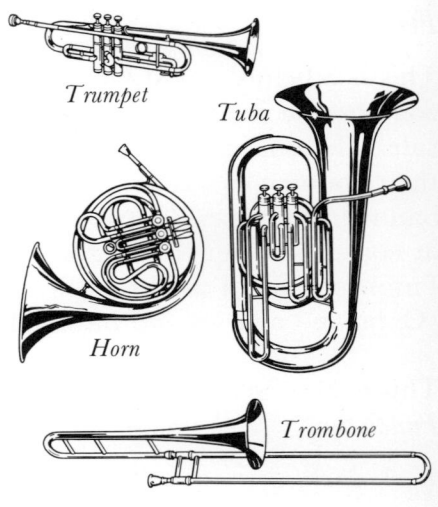

Trumpet

Tuba

Horn

Trombone

Intermezzo
This music begins with one of Sibelius's favourite effects – strings played *tremolando* ('trembling') with swift up-and-down movements of the bow. Against this rustling background, we hear mysterious horn calls. The music builds up. Then this lively tune bursts out on trumpets above an exciting accompaniment:

Eventually the music quietens, and the horn calls are heard once more. At the very end, as one horn sinks lower, another soars up to almost the highest note it can play.

Alla Marcia
The title of this rousing piece means 'in the style of a march'. There are two tunes, **A** and **B**:

A[1]	violins
B[1]	first, trumpets; then trombones and tuba with trumpet fanfares
A[2]	woodwind
B[2]	horns, trombones and tuba with trumpet fanfares
A[3]	violins
Coda	a 'rounding-off' – using a snatch from each tune

On the right you can see how Sibelius builds up the music of his march, using tune **A** and **B** alternately.

Finale, from Symphony No. 5 in E flat major

Sibelius's *Fifth Symphony* is made up of three movements (or separate pieces). The final movement is marked *Allegro molto*, meaning 'very quickly'.

The music begins with strings played *tremolando* ('trembling') suggesting, perhaps, the wind rustling through the Finnish forests:

Gradually, the other instruments of the orchestra join in. After the music has grown louder, this swinging, bell-like tune is played by the horns:

As the horns continue to play Tune **B**, another tune rides above it, played by the woodwind:

Both these tunes, **B** and **C**, are played again, now with the full orchestra involved, and with richer, glowing harmonies.

Then Sibelius puts together a musical jigsaw made up of scraps of Tunes **A**, **B** and **C**.

Later, we hear the strings playing the same rustling music as at the beginning of the movement (Tune **A**). Sibelius now marks their music *misterioso* – 'mysteriously'.

Listen for Tunes **B** and **C** to return on strings and woodwind. Violins then sing a broader, slower version of Tune **C**. From this, the swinging, bell-like tune (**B**) – now played mainly by the trumpets – takes the music to a powerful, majestic climax.

Then Sibelius ends his Symphony with six widely-spaced, hammered chords.

The orchestra needed to play Sibelius's *Fifth Symphony* includes:

2 flutes	2 clarinets
2 oboes	2 bassoons
4 horns	3 trombones
3 trumpets	

kettle drums (timpani)

first violins	cellos
second violins	double basses
violas	

BÉLA BARTÓK

1881–1945   HUNGARY (died in U.S.A.)

Béla Bartók

Borders between countries in Eastern Europe are often changing. Bartók was born in a corner of Hungary which is now counted as part of Romania. He received his first piano lessons from his mother at the age of five, and gave his first concert when he was ten. By this time, he was already composing. Later, he became a student at the Academy of Music in Budapest.

Bartók became friends with another Hungarian composer, Zoltán Kodály. Both composers took a keen interest in the study of Hungarian folk-tunes. They suspected that the gypsy tunes, usually accepted as typical Hungarian folk-music, were very different from the tunes of the true Hungarian peasant folk. They visited many remote villages – not only in Hungary, but in Romania, Bulgaria, and other neighbouring countries as well. Sometimes they wrote down the tunes they heard; sometimes they took with them a recording machine and made recordings of the tunes as they were sung or played. Between them they collected more than six thousand folk-tunes.

Many of these folk-tunes were in very irregular rhythms which sometimes changed from one bar to the next. Few of them used our normal major or minor scales, and some suggested rather strange harmonies. Bartók studied these tunes closely. He made arrangements of many of them; others he used to build up larger pieces of music. Of course, Bartók does not include folk-tunes in all his compositions. But even when the music is entirely of his own invention, his tunes and rhythms carry a strong flavour of the peasant tunes he had studied.

Copyright G.D. Hackett, N.Y.

Bartók recording a peasant woman singing a folksong

Bartók frequently spices his music with strong discords. A tune and its accompaniment may be in two different keys at once. In his piano music, Bartók often emphasises the brightly percussive sound which the piano can make, and encourages the pianist to use a steely, brilliant tone. (Quite the opposite, in fact, to the French composer, Debussy, who said that in many of *his* pieces, the pianist should try to imagine 'an instrument without hammers'.)

Romanian Folk Dances

These are all peasant fiddle-tunes which Bartók recorded in remote, isolated villages in that region of Romania known as Transylvania.

In 1915, he arranged them as a group of six dances for piano. He called them: Stick dance, Sash dance, In one spot, Horn dance, Romanian Polka, and Fast dance. Two years later, Bartók made a version for small orchestra – now making the sixth dance into two short separate dances, both sharing the same title.

Here are the first two dances, and then the opening tune of each of the other five:

Bartók

Third movement from Sonata for Two Pianos and Percussion

Bartók composed this music in 1937 when he was living in Budapest, the capital city of Hungary. When the piece was first performed, Bartók himself played the first piano part and his wife, Ditta, played the second.

Two percussion players are needed in a performance of Bartók's Sonata. These percussion instruments are shared between them:

3 pedal-tuned kettle drums
xylophone (in which bars of wood, graded in length, are hit with beaters)
1 side drum, with snares
1 side drum, with the snares lifted away from the drumskin
pair of cymbals (clashed)
suspended cymbals (hit with various kinds of sticks)
bass drum
triangle
tam tam (a large gong)

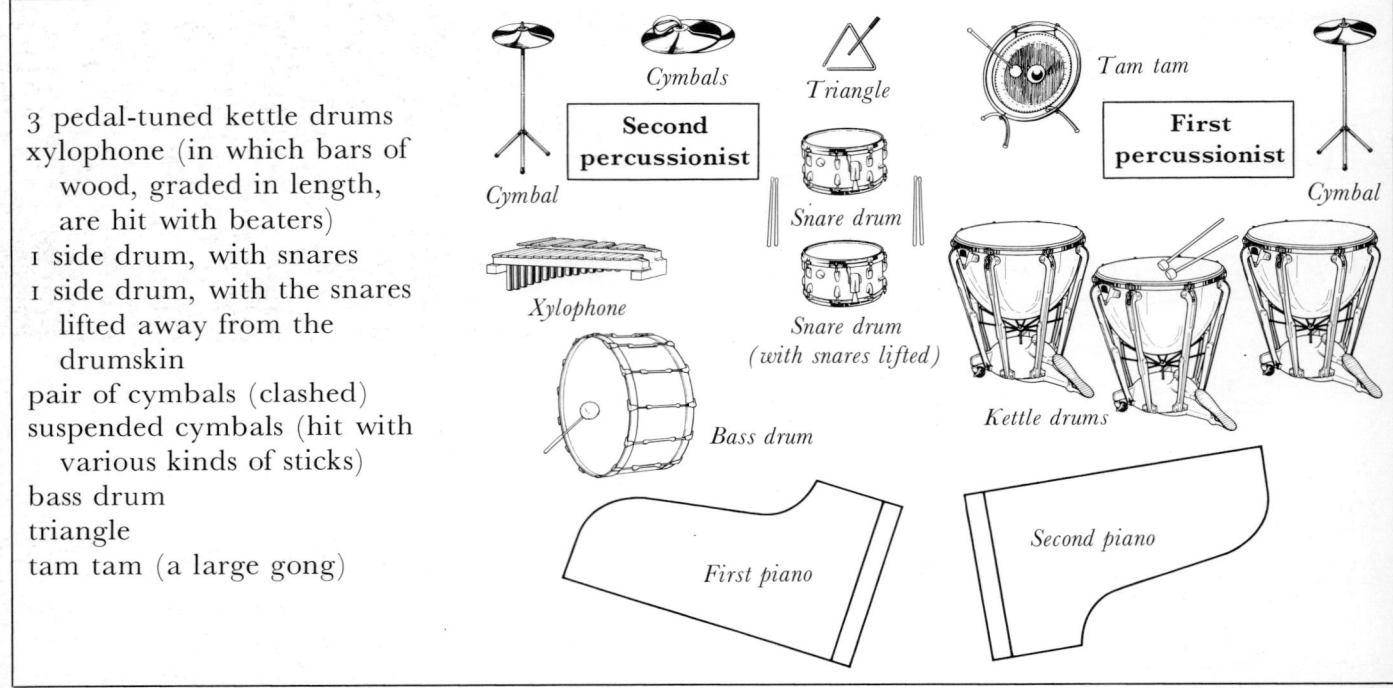

Bartók's *Sonata for Two Pianos and Percussion* is in three movements. The tunes and rhythms of the third movement make the music sound like a lively folk-dance – but in fact, Bartók uses no folk-tunes in this piece at all. The music is vigorous and exciting, and Bartók draws a rich variety of sound-colours from his group of instruments.

The main tune is first played by the xylophone, with kettle drum notes filling in the gaps:

Listen for other percussion instruments to join in: cymbals, triangle, snare drum – and later, bass drum.

In the central section of the movement, which begins after a pause, Bartók breaks up his main tune into fragments (marked with brackets above the tune). Sometimes we hear these fragments played upside down, or even backwards.

Later, the music becomes more vigorous still. Then towards the end, as a rhythm is repeatedly tapped out on a snare drum, it slows down. The final sounds on the cymbal are made by touching the edge with the blade of a penknife.

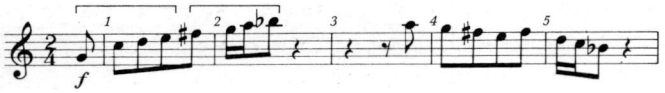

First movement ('Verbunkos') from 'Contrasts'

In 1938, Bartók was asked by the American jazz clarinettist, Benny Goodman, to write a piece for clarinet, violin and piano. Bartók himself was to play the piano part, and his friend, Josef Szigeti, was to be the violinist.

At first, Bartók could not see how he might blend together three instruments which make their sounds in such very different ways. He decided to do exactly the opposite – instead of trying to blend the sounds and tone-colours, he would contrast them one against the another. And so he called the music *Contrasts*.

Although much of Bartók's music is based on the style and flavour of the genuine folk-tunes he discovered, he chose to compose the first movement of *Contrasts* in the style of Hungarian gypsy music. Gypsy bands usually included as their main instruments the clarinet and the violin. When the Hungarian Army wanted to attract new recruits it would organise evenings of merry-making in the villages, with music played by a gypsy band. One of the dances was the *verbunkos*, which means 'recruiting dance'.

Bartók's *Verbunkos* begins with a short, crisp introduction played by the violin and piano. Then the main tune is heard on the clarinet:

Later on, listen for a rather sad tune to be played by the violin in Hungarian gypsy style:

At the end of the piece, the clarinet has a *cadenza*. Here, violin and piano are silent while the clarinettist plays a very difficult, florid solo.

The clarinet

This woodwind instrument has a single reed – a flat piece of cane fixed to the mouthpiece by a metal band. The player's breath causes this reed to vibrate (rather like a piece of grass held between the thumbs and blown).

The lower notes of the clarinet sound rather hollow, but rich and velvety. In the middle register, the sound is smooth, while in the higher register the tone can be very piercing. The clarinet has a very wide range of expression.

In the *Verbunkos* by Bartók, the piano mainly provides an accompaniment. But the clarinet and violin are given difficult, often spectacular, music to play. Listen for *contrasts* between the varied sounds these instruments make:

Clarinet: rapid scales, trills, arpeggios (the notes of a chord spread out and played one after another)

changes in tone-quality between low notes and high notes, and between *fortissimo* (very loud) and *pianissimo* (very soft)

Violin: *pizzicato* (plucked notes) and *arco* (bowed notes)

double stoppings – making two strings sound at once

PERCY GRAINGER

1882–1961 AUSTRALIA (died in U.S.A.)

music. Most composers use Italian words to tell performers how their music should be played. Grainger is more likely to use English. Instead of *crescendo* he will write 'louden lots'; or instead of *rallentando*, 'slow off'. He may ask a pianist to play 'clingingly', 'clangingly', or 'bumpily'!

Grainger became a close friend of the Norwegian composer Grieg, and often stayed at his home near Bergen. He also frequently visited the English composer Delius, who had settled in a small town not far from Paris. Later, Delius was to become blind and paralysed, but Grainger always cheered up the household considerably with his humorous tricks. One of his favourites – which never failed to astound guests taking tea in the garden – was to hurl a ball high over the roof, then dash madly right through the house to catch it before it fell at the other side!

Percy Grainger was born in Melbourne. He first took up a career as a concert pianist, but later he became known more as a composer. He travelled widely, visiting New Zealand, Central Europe, Scandinavia and Africa. In 1901 he settled for a time in England. Then in 1914 he went to live permanently in America, taking up American citizenship four years later.

Many of Grainger's pieces are arrangements of folk-songs and dances, which he collected keenly wherever he went. Several of his compositions are published in different versions. For instance, the same piece may be arranged for piano solo, for a group of a dozen or so instruments, for wind band, and also for full orchestra.

Grainger had a lively sense of humour, and this often shows in the comments he writes on his

Grainger, with the blind composer Delius and his wife, Jelka

Country Gardens

This became the most popular of all Grainger's pieces. It is an arrangement of a morris dance-tune which Grainger came across when he was living in England. A morris dance is performed by men only. They wear tiny bells tied around their legs, and carry sticks or handkerchiefs.

Country Gardens has three tunes. All three are heard closely following one another at the beginning of the piece:

Grainger dedicated *Country Gardens* to the memory of his friend, the Norwegian composer, Edvard Grieg.

Two other pieces by Grainger are in morris dance style: *Shepherd's Hey* (which, like *Country Gardens*, is based on a genuine morris dance-tune); and the lively *Mock Morris*, in which the tunes are all of Grainger's own invention.

Morris dancing in an English village

Brigg Fair

This is a very old English folk-song which Grainger heard at the small town of Brigg in Lincolnshire. The song had been sung at Brigg for a great many years, passed on from one generation to the next. No one knew who had originally made up the song. Over the years, both tune and words must have been changed slightly here and there, as is often the case with folk-songs. Grainger arranged *Brigg Fair* for solo tenor (a high-sounding male voice) and a choir of mixed voices. The music is sung without any accompaniment. Here is the first verse of *Brigg Fair:*

2.
I rose up with the lark in the morning
    With 'my heart so full of glee,
Of thinking there to meet my dear
    Long time I wished to see.

3.
I took hold of her lily-white hand,
    And merrily was her heart,
And now we're met together,
    I hope we ne'er shall part.

4.
For it's meeting is a pleasure
    And parting is a grief
But an unconstant lover
    Is worse than a thief.

5.
The green leaves they shall wither
    And the branches they shall die
If ever I prove false to her
    To the girl that loves me.

The solo tenor sings the words of verses 1 to 3 while the choir is heard humming quiet chords in the background. In verse 4, the choir sings the words – but the tenor joins in part of the way through with an anguished cry of 'Ah!'. The tenor sings the last verse – accompanied, as at the beginning, by quiet chords hummed by the choir.

Soon after he had written this piece, Grainger went to France to visit his friend, Delius. He let Delius hear *Brigg Fair*. Delius was so attracted by the tune that, a year later, he used it in one of his own pieces. Delius's *Brigg Fair* is a set of variations for orchestra based on the same tune.

SERGEY PROKOFIEV

1891–1953   U.S.S.R.

Prokofiev was writing his first piano pieces when he was five, and composed a short opera when he was eight. At thirteen, he became a student at the Conservatoire in St. Petersburg (the city now known as Leningrad). One of his teachers was the famous Russian composer, Rimsky-Korsakov. By the time Prokofiev had completed his musical studies, he had already made a name as a composer and pianist.

Prokofiev left Russia at the time of the Russian Revolution. He travelled the world, passing through Siberia, Japan and Honolulu, and stayed for two years in America. Then he settled in Paris. Much of his music at that time did not greatly attract people. It was very rhythmic, and colourfully orchestrated – but audiences complained that it sounded too harsh and that Prokofiev could not write a good tune. In 1932, he returned to Russia, and the music he composed then (which includes *Peter and the Wolf* and the ballet *Romeo and Juliet*) is much more mellow and tuneful.

Third Movement from Symphony No. 1 in D major (the 'Classical')

Prokofiev was twenty-five when he composed his first symphony. He called it the 'Classical' because he deliberately set out to make the music sound similar in style to symphonies by Classical composers such as Haydn and Mozart. Prokofiev uses an orchestra of the same size, and the rhythms of the music have a similar grace and elegance. But he frequently takes a tune and gives it a sudden twist, sending it into an unexpected key. This gives the music a flavour which is very definitely of the 20th century.

The third movement of Prokofiev's *'Classical' Symphony* is a *gavotte* – a very dignified dance which was popular during the 18th century. Prokofiev shapes this movement in *ternary* form:
Tune **A** – Tune **B** – Tune **A** again.

Prokofiev

Peter and the Wolf – A Musical Tale for Children

In *Peter and the Wolf*, Prokofiev presents a story in both words and music. Each character taking part is represented by one or more instruments of the orchestra – rather like the actors in a play. So as we listen to the story, we come to recognise the special sounds of these different instruments. Before the story begins, Prokofiev introduces us to the characters, one by one.

The high, chirruping music of the Bird is played by the flute:

Flute

The melancholy tune of the Duck is played by the oboe:

Oboe

The stealthy, stalking tune of the Cat is played by the clarinet – in its lower register, where the notes sound dark and velvety rich:

Clarinet

The tune of Peter's rather grumpy old Grandfather is played, low down in the bass, by the bassoon:

Bassoon

The Wolf's music is played by three horns:

Horns

Peter – the brave young hero of the story – is represented by all the string instruments of the orchestra. This is Peter's tune:

Double bass

Viola

Violin

Cello

Later in the story, we hear the gunshots of the Hunters crashing out on the kettle drums and the big, bass drum:

Bass drum

(kettle drums)

(bass drum)

Kettle drums

Once we have been introduced to these instruments and their tunes, Prokofiev unfolds his story in words and music.

AARON COPLAND

Born 1900 U.S.A.

A. Copland

Aaron Copland, America's most important 20th century composer, was born in Brooklyn, New York. He first studied music in New York and then, for three years, in France. Returning to America in 1924, Copland had very clear ideas about the kind of music he wanted to compose:

> 'When I returned to New York after my musical studies in Europe, I definitely set out to write music which everyone could understand was American.'

Copland brings an American flavour to many of his pieces by using rhythms borrowed from jazz, and by including American folksongs. This is especially true of three ballets he has written called *Billy the Kid*, *Rodeo*, and *Appalachian Spring*.

Suite from the ballet: 'Billy the Kid'

Billy the Kid (real name – William H. Bonney) lived from 1859 to 1881. He was born in New York but, as a boy, joined a group of pioneers making the trek to the West.

For a time, Billy lived in Silver City, New Mexico. By the age of eighteen, he was leader of a gang of cattle rustlers – and was already wanted for murder.

Billy's very brief but violent career as an outlawed bandit and killer quickly made him into one of the fabulous legends of the American Southwest. Countless stories – many of them untrue – were told of his crimes and adventures. He was said to have notches on his pistol boasting of twenty-one killings. And though he was captured many times, he always managed to escape – until, at the age of twenty-two, he met his death at the hands of Pat Garrett, Sheriff of Lincoln County, and Billy's one-time friend.

Billy the Kid

REWARD

($5,000.00)

Reward for the capture, dead or alive,
of one Wm. Wright, better known as

"BILLY THE KID"

Age, 18. Height, 5 feet, 3 inches.
Weight, 125 lbs. Light hair, blue
eyes and even features. He is
the leader of the worst band of
desperadoes the Territory has
ever had to deal with. The above
reward will be paid for his capture
or positive proof of his death.
JIM DALTON, Sheriff.

DEAD OR ALIVE!
"BILLY THE KID"

Here is Copland's own description of the story of his ballet, *Billy the Kid*:

'The action begins and closes on the open prairie. The central portion of the ballet concerns itself with the significant moments in the life of Billy the Kid.

The first scene is a street in a frontier town. Familiar figures amble by. Cowboys saunter into town, some on horseback, others with their lassoes. Some Mexican women dance a *jarabe* which is interrupted by a fight between two drunks. Attracted by the gathering crowd, Billy is seen for the first time as a boy of twelve with his mother. The brawl turns ugly, guns are drawn, and in some unaccountable way, Billy's mother is killed. Without an instant's hesitation, in cold fury, Billy draws a knife from a cowhand's sheath and stabs his mother's slayers. His short but famous career has begun.

In swift succession, we see episodes from Billy's later life. At night, under the stars, in a quiet card game with his outlaw friends. Hunted by a posse led by his former friend, Pat Garrett, Billy is pursued. A running battle ensues. Billy is captured. A drunken celebration takes place. Billy in prison is, of course, followed by one of Billy's legendary escapes.

Tired and worn in the desert, Billy rests with his girl. Starting from a deep sleep, he senses movement in the shadows. The posse has finally caught up with him. It is the end.'

In the music for his ballet, *Billy the Kid*, Copland uses several American cowboy songs, including 'Great Grandad', 'Old Paint', 'The Old Chisholm Trail', 'The Dying Cowboy' and 'Riding Free'.

As you will hear, these songs do not appear note for note. Copland often alters the rhythm of the tunes, and even the melody-notes themselves. 'I can't imagine Billy without these cowboy tunes,' says Copland. 'Of course, what I hoped to do was to give these tunes my own flavour.'

Copland's ballet was very successful. Later, he selected some of the music to make a *suite*. This does not cover the entire story of the ballet, but brings together seven sections of the music:

1. The Open Prairie

This music creates a fresh, outdoor atmosphere. Copland builds up a musical picture of the vast, open spaces of the prairie lands in the Southwest of America.

2. Street in a Frontier Town

Here are some of the tunes which Copland uses in this quite lengthy second section of his Suite:

('Paint' comes from the Spanish, *pinto*, meaning horse.)

3. Card Game at Night (Prairie Night)

Soft, peaceful night-music. Flute and violins are the main instruments. Later, there is a solo for trumpet.

4. Gun Battle

A running battle which ends in Billy's capture. Wild, jagged rhythms on percussion instruments and harsh chords for the brass.

5. Celebration after Billy's Capture

Gay, jaunty music – colourful sounds from wind and percussion.

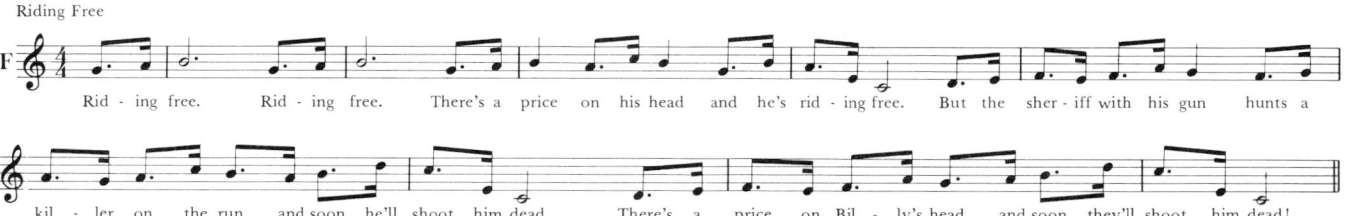

Riding Free

Rid - ing free. Rid - ing free. There's a price on his head and he's rid - ing free. But the sher - iff with his gun hunts a kil - ler on the run and soon he'll shoot him dead. There's a price on Bil - ly's head and soon they'll shoot him dead!

6. Billy's Death

A quiet lament, played mainly by the string section of the orchestra.

7. The Open Prairie

A return to the music of the opening section, Tune **A**, which builds up to a menacing climax on the full orchestra.

Variations on a Shaker song, from the ballet 'Appalachian Spring'

The story of this ballet takes place in the hills of Pennsylvania during the 19th century. It tells of a group of settlers who hold a celebration in springtime around a newly-built farmhouse. The two main characters in the ballet are a young farmer and the girl who shortly becomes his bride.

About three-quarters of the way through the ballet, Copland writes five variations on a song borrowed from the Shaker religion, called 'Simple Gifts'. As these variations are played, the newly-married couple are shown carrying out daily tasks on their new farm. The Shaker tune is first played by a solo clarinet:

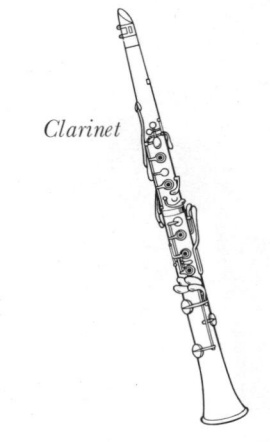

Clarinet

This is what happens to the tune in the variations:
1. The tune is played slightly faster by oboe and bassoon.
2. The first half of the tune only, twice as slowly, on violas and trombones. Violins and horns come in with the tune later.
3. A very lively variation for trumpets and trombones against swift, scurrying passages for violins and violas.
4. The second half of the tune only, flowing, on the woodwind.
5. For the full orchestra – broadly, and triumphantly. The tune rides proudly above rich, striding chords, and each main beat is punched out strongly on the drums.

BENJAMIN BRITTEN

1913–1976 ENGLAND

Many people think of Benjamin Britten as one of the very greatest 20th century composers. He was born in Lowestoft, Suffolk, on St. Cecilia's day, which is November 22nd. (St. Cecilia is the patron saint of music.) By the time he was twelve, Britten had already composed several pieces. He then began to take lessons from the composer, Frank Bridge. Later, he became a student at the Royal College of Music.

After leaving college, Britten worked for a while in England, then in 1939 he went to live in America. But as World War II progressed, he began to feel strongly that his rightful place was in his own country. So in 1942, he returned to England, eventually settling in Aldeburgh, a small fishing town on the Suffolk coast. It was here that he composed his first important opera, *Peter Grimes*, which is a tragic drama about the sea and fisherfolk. In 1948, Britten founded the Aldeburgh Festival at which concerts are held each summer featuring performances of his compositions.

Britten had a deep love and understanding for the human voice, and a marvellous sensitivity in setting words to music. Among his many vocal compositions – besides his operas – are the *Serenade* for tenor, horn and strings, *Ceremony of Carols*, *Spring Symphony*, and the deeply moving *War Requiem*, composed for the opening of the newly-built Coventry Cathedral in 1962.

Britten was interested, too, in writing music for young people. He introduces them to opera in *Let's Make an Opera* and *Noyes Fludde*, and to the instruments of the orchestra in *A Young Person's Guide to the Orchestra*.

Whereas many 20th century composers have tried new, and sometimes rather strange, techniques in writing their music, Britten has always made use of the familiar musical ingredients used by other great composers before him. He may often mix these ingredients together in unexpected, even surprising ways – but the results always sound fresh, imaginative, totally convincing.

A scene from the opera 'Noyes Fludde'

Music from 'Serenade' for tenor, horn and strings

Britten's *Serenade* consists of settings of poems by six English poets. Each poem is in some way connected with thoughts of evening or nightfall – the glowing haze of sunset, mysterious lengthenings of shadows, the coming of darkness, and sleep.

First, there is a *Prologue* for horn alone. Britten asks the player not to use the valves, but to play 'natural harmonics' – that is, to produce all the notes by lip pressure only. Here is the beginning of this horn solo:

The horn

The first kind of horn to be used in the orchestra was a smaller version of the hunting horn. A length of tubing was coiled into a circle, with a mouthpiece at one end, and a wide 'bell' at the other. Like the early trumpet, it could play only those notes available from a single length of tubing – except horn players found that a few extra notes could be made by adjusting the hand inside the bell. The total length of the tube could be altered by changing 'crooks'. These were extra loops of tubing, graded in size. But though a different crook provided a new *range* of notes, the actual *number* available was exactly the same.

An early horn, with crooks

Then around 1820, the 'modern' horn with three valves came into use. (This is sometimes called the 'French horn', possibly because of its early use in France.) The valves do the work of the old-fashioned crooks – they add in extra bits of tubing at the touch of a finger. So by using the valves, and altering the pressure of his lips, the horn player can play a complete range of notes.

mouthpiece

The player supports the instrument by resting his right hand lightly inside the bell. The tone of the horn is usually round and mellow, but if the player pushes his hand well inside the bell and blows hard it can sound very brassy. A pear-shaped *mute* can be inserted into the bell. This makes the tone sound thinner, more metallic, and as if coming from the distance.

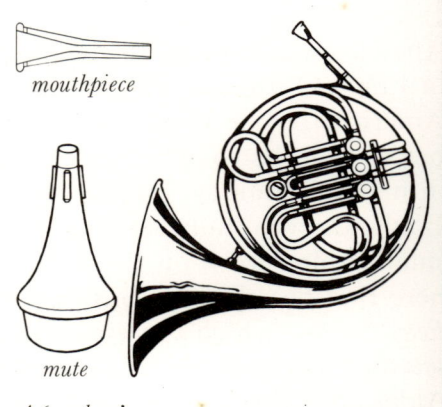

mute

A 'modern' horn, with valves

Nocturne

The poem which Britten sets to music here is by the 19th century poet, Alfred, Lord Tennyson. At the close of each verse, a rustling chord is held by the strings. Above this, voice and horn echo and answer each other:

For the second verse the horn is muted so that the sound becomes distant, mysterious, slightly menacing.

> The splendour falls on castle walls
> And snowy summits old in story:
> The long night shakes across the lakes,
> And the wild cataract leaps in glory:
>
> Blow, bugle, blow, set the wild echoes flying,
> Bugle, blow; answer, echoes, answer, dying.
>
> O hark, O hear, how thin and clear,
> And thinner, clearer, farther going!
> O sweet and far from cliff and scar
> The horns of elfland faintly blowing!
>
> Blow, let us hear the purple glens replying:
> Bugle, blow; answer, echoes, answer, dying.
>
> O love, they die in yon rich sky,
> They faint on hill or field or river:
> Our echoes roll from soul to soul
> And grow for ever and for ever.
>
> Blow, bugle, blow, set the wild echoes flying;
> And answer, echoes, answer, dying.

Hymn

This poem – by the Elizabethan poet, Ben Jonson – is a hymn to Diana, the goddess of hunting. In some legends, however, Diana represents the moon, and Jonson brings together both these ideas in his poem.

Britten's music is swift, light and deftly rhythmic. It requires the greatest skill and musicianship from both singer and horn player. The strings are played *pizzicato* throughout.

> Queen and huntress, chaste and fair,
> Now the sun is laid to sleep,
> Seated in thy silver chair,
> State in wonted manner keep:
> Hesperus entreats thy light,
> Goddess excellently bright.
>
> Earth, let not thy envious shade
> Dare itself to interpose;
> Cynthia's shining orb was made,
> Heav'n to clear when day did close:
> Bless us then with wishèd sight,
> Goddess excellently bright.
>
> Lay thy bow of pearl apart,
> And thy crystal shining quiver;
> Give unto the flying hart
> Space to breathe, how short so-ever:
> Thou that mak'st a day of night,
> Goddess excellently bright.